Telelearning via the Internet

Rafa Kouki
University of Ottawa

David Wright
University of Ottawa

IDEA GROUP PUBLISHING
Hershey USA • London UK

Senior Editor: Mehdi Khosrowpour
Managing Editor: Jan Travers
Copy Editor: John Syphryt
Cover Design: Marjane Talebi
Printed at: BookCrafters

Published in the United States of America by
        Idea Group Publishing
        1331 E. Chocolate Avenue
        Hershey PA 17033-1117
        Tel: 717-533-8845
        Fax: 717-533-8661
        E-mail: jtravers@idea-group.com
        Website: http://www.idea-group.com

and in the United Kingdom by
        Idea Group Publishing
        3 Henrietta Street
        Covent Garden
        London WC2E 8LU
        Tel: 171-240 0856
        Fax: 171-379 0609
        Website: http://www.eurospan.co.uk

Library of Congress Cataloging-in-Publication Data

Kouki, Rafa
        Telelearning via the Internet/Rafa Kouki, David Wright.
        p.   cm.
        Includes index.
        ISBN 1-878289-53-5
        1. Distance education. 2. Teaching--Computer network resources. 3. Internet
(Computer network) in education. 4. Education--Computer network resources. I.
Wright, David, 1947- . II. Title.
LC5800.K68 1999   98-42754
378.1 ' 7344678--dc21   CIP

British Cataloguing in Publication Data
A Cataloguing in Publication record for this book is available from the British Library.

To Rafa Kouki's parents, Feten, Sonia and Haythem

To David Wright's wife, Mina,
daughter, Leila, and son, Ramin

Thank you for your encouragement and support

Telelearning via the Internet

Table of Contents

Preface

The largest and most powerful computer network in the world, the public Internet has brought about momentous changes in the way we create, store, disseminate and acquire knowledge. Being one of the first areas to be influenced by these revolutionary transformations, the academic environment has been witnessing the rise of a new form of teaching and transferring knowledge: telelearning via the Internet. Internet-based telelearning is increasing in popularity among the Internet community. Already hundreds of on-line courses and degrees are offered by conventional and virtual educational institutions. The Internet's flexibility, robustness, wide reach and low cost, are the main drivers for this new means of delivering education.

This book:

- describes the tools required for telelearning via the Internet,
- provides examples of how educational institutions are using those tools,
- identifies the benefits of different options for accessing the Internet and
- highlights the major current issues: Internet security, copyright of digital material, and accreditation of on-line degrees and programs.

The book is in four parts. Part I includes a description of a variety of synchronous and asynchronous Internet tools, as well as their advantages and drawbacks for educational applications. In part II, case studies of Internet-based telelearning applications are described, in addition to a discussion of the results of two investigations about the current implementations of Internet tools within a telelearning setting. Part III provides an analysis of the alternative Internet access options and their costs related to both the students and the educational institutions. Part IV presents the open issues which currently face educators and students on the Internet including security and educational policy concerns.

Acronyms Used in This Book

ADSL	: Asymmetric Digital Subscriber Line.
B-channel	: Bearer Channel.
BRI	: Basic Rate ISDN.
CGI	: Common Gateway Interface.
CSU	: Channel Service Unit.
D-channel	: Data Channel.
DEOS-L	: Distance Education On-line Symposium Listserv
DNS	: Domain Name Server.
DSU	: Data Service Unit.
FTP	: File Transfer Protocol.
GIF	: Graphics Interchange Format.
HTML	: Hypertext Markup Language.
HTTP	: Hypertext Transfer Protocol.
HTTPS	: Secure Hypertext Transport Protocol.
IMM	: Image Multicaster
IP	: Internet Protocol.
IRC	: Internet Relay Chat.
ISDN	: Integrated Services Digital Network.
ISP	: Internet Service Provider.
Kbps	: Kilobits per second.
MBONE	: Multicast backBONE.
Mbps	: Mega bits per second.
MIME	: Multipurpose Internet Mail Extensions.
MOO	: Object-Oriented MUD.
Mrouter	: Multicast router.
MUD	: Multi User Dimensions.
Nevot	: Network Voice Terminal.
NV	: Net Video.
PDF	: Portable Document Format.
PEM	: Privacy Enhanced Mail.
PGP	: Pretty Good Privacy.
POTS	: Plain Old Telephone Service.
PPP	: Point to Point Protocol.
PRI	: Primary Rate ISDN.
QoS	: Quality of Service
RSVP	: Resource reSerVation Protocol.
RTP	: Real Time Protocol.
SLIP	: Serial Line Internet Protocol.
SSL	: Secure Socket Layer.
TCP	: Transmission Control Protocol.
TTL	: Time To Live.
VAT	: Visual Audio Tool.
VRML	: Virtual Reality Modeling Language.
UDP	: User Datagram Protocol.
WB	: WhiteBoard.
WWW	: World Wide Web.

Part I

■

Internet Tools

Part I of this book provides a description of the vast range of Internet tools, which can be used to create a telelearning environment. These tools fall into two main categories: those which provide asynchronous communications and others which allow for real time interaction. They are covered in two chapters: Chapter 1: which discusses the main Internet asynchronous tools and Chapter 2 which describes synchronous or real time tools.

Asynchronous communications is based on messaging where the participants do not have to be connected to the Internet simultaneously. Real time communications is based on live conferencing in which all participants are simultaneously connected to the Internet session.

Each chapter provides a description of the tool or the technology and its different features, its advantages, its limitations and problems, and a description of how it is being implemented for on-line lectures, or how it can be used in the near future.

Popular tools have not been described in detail. Instead, emphasis was on their advantages and limitations and on the recent developments and additions which can improve on-line interactive environments. Other tools such as CUSeeMe and the MBONE, are also described in detail.

Chapter 1

■

Asynchronous Communication Tools

Electronic Mail

Electronic mail is an asynchronous method of telecommunication, which allows users to post private, individual or group messages. E-mail is the most popular Internet application and many educational institutions having access to the Internet are heavily using it to provide support for their regular courses for information exchange among students and instructors.

The reasons why e-mail is so popular can be explained by the following:

- It is easy to use and just requires a simple Internet connection.
- Messages are quickly delivered, which allows for better communication between students and instructors, facilitates receipt of important course material and speeds up feedback.
- E-mail has many interesting features which allow for group collaboration such as message forwarding.
- It is not time or place dependent and messages can be accessed at any time. This makes communication more flexible, as it increases the instructor's availability and allows class discussions to extend beyond the regular class time. The asynchronous feature of the e-mail, provides students with more time to think about an appropriate answer, and to phrase their responses more carefully than would be possible in a situation where an immediate answer is required. Such extended and better organized discussions can be very helpful for easier assimilation of the material.
- It is a low cost method of contacting people in different parts of the world.

This brings opportunities to class members to reach experts and other students around the world.

• The Multipurpose Internet Mail Extensions MIME, enables multimedia attachments.

• New browsers combine HTML and e-mail so that a sender can include links to several web links in the message. This feature is very useful in a telelearning environment, where an instructor can support an answer to a student's question, by links and references to Web documents.

E-mail, on the other hand has several limitations, which restrict its use as basic tool for telelearning and limit its use as a support tool to on-line lectures. These limitations in some of the cases, can outweigh the advantages of this tool, if it is to be used as the primary tool for on-line lectures.

Despite the advantages of the option of sending multimedia files as attachments to messages, the different encoding methods used can cause several problems to the receiver as well as to the sender. Before sending a file attachment over the Internet using e-mail, certain points should be taken into consideration.

There are two common encoding methods for email attachments - MIME (Multiple Internet Mail Extension) and UUENCODE. Most Internet e-mail software (like MS Exchange, Netscape Mail, or Eudora) already integrates one of these encoding methods into its file attachment functionality.

Several other encoding schemes exist, however. If a user receives an e-mail attachment encoded using different method, the attached file can't be automatically converted because of the difference in encoding methods. Therefore, the user needs to manually convert (decode) the e-mail's attached file back to its original format.

In order to prevent such problems in a telelearning environment, on-line class members can agree on a standard for the course. This can be sometimes difficult, because every student needs to have an application, which supports the encoding system.

As stated earlier, e-mail can be used to send several types of files, including graphics and pictures. Animation, sound, graphical and picture files are usually very large. The larger the file, the longer it will take students to download their e-mail with such attachments. Moreover, in order to retrieve, and execute such files, students require a lot of disk space. The sender, either the instructor or a student, should inform the receiver(s) before sending messages with long attachments. There are several other methods to expand basic e-mail functions and to organize discussions about topics in a telelearning class, including mailing lists, listservs and newsgroups.

Mailing lists-Listservs

Mailing lists allow the redistribution of an e-mail to a list of subscribed addresses. Mailing lists have normally a subject about which participants can make announcements and discussions. Mailing lists, therefore, can provide a useful way for teachers interested in specific topics to communicate with others who share the same interests.

There are several types of mailing lists. A "moderated" mailing list is one where only the list owner or moderator receives all the messages and then decides whether to forward them to the subscribers. Moderate mailing lists fit very well for on-line class discussions, where a mailing list for the class can be set up, with the instructor as the moderator and students as the other participants.

"One way" mailing lists, which do not expect replies from receivers, can also be used jointly with moderated lists, to post announcements or news to the students.

"Public" or "open" mailing lists, provide an opportunity for students to get in touch with worldwide experts in the field they are interested in and with other students from different schools and countries.

Mailing lists provide users with the same features as the basic e-mail such as different file attachments and mail forwarding. One popular program used to manage mailing lists is called "listserv" which has become synonymous to mailing lists.

Some of the limitations of mailing lists include:

- It can be hard to follow the thread of a discussion. Participants need to specify the subject very clearly in their replies.
- They need to be continuously managed. That is e-mail should be regularly read and irrelevant messages should be deleted, otherwise the users' mailbox can be overwhelmed. This can be very time consuming, especially if the mailing list is very large.
- Because of the overwhelming e-mail, it is difficult for a user to subscribe to several mailing lists at the same time. This therefore, can limit the opportunities for students interested in several subjects to take part in several discussions.

Newsgroups

Newsgroups, also referred to as Usenet news, are another e-mail application which allows several people to discuss and exchange messages and files. Each newsgroup has a specific topic. Unlike mailing lists, users do not have to manage their incoming mail. With newsgroups, a newsreader should be used. The software's main function is to manage the incoming messages and to display them in threads. Having a thread of messages means that a message and all its replies are linked together, making it easy for a reader to follow an entire discussion. This constitutes a very important advantage over mailing lists and regular e-mail.

The reasons why instructors and students use Usenet news are very similar to those for using mailing lists. Usenet news can be very effective in case students want to participate in several newsgroups with different subjects, but cannot easily manage the overwhelming number of email messages that mailing lists generate.

Newsgroups are usually focused about specific topics. It is, therefore, easier to find newsgroups of interest to the class than using public mailing lists. As mentioned above, the "threads" option makes it easier for students to follow the flow of a discussion and to see what others contributed to a specific topic, an important feature for out of class discussions.

One other important advantage of newsgroups compared with mailing lists, is that messages are available on-line from a few days to a few weeks. Mailing list messages, on the other hand, are not stored anywhere on-line. This feature helps students to know whether the questions they want to ask have been recently asked and answered or not. Also, if students want to join a public newsgroup, the instructor can tell whether it is appropriate for their interests or not, by reviewing the discussions of the chosen newsgroup.

One important thing to note, though, is the lack of control over the posted material. Inappropriate material may be contributed to newsgroups. If a school teacher is planning to provide newsgroup access to minors, he/she can investigate the software programs designed to allow parents and educators to limit student's Internet access. In many cases, instructors might want to screen out certain messages during a discussion. With a "kill file", the instructor can set the newsreader software to ignore articles by specific people.

Multimedia for E-mail

Adding multimedia to e-mail is of great benefit to users of this tool, including educational institutions. A multimedia e-mail message can include still images, audio and video clips. In an educational environment, adding fonts, color characters, graphics and audio and video clips adds value to the received message especially when used for courses where such support materials are fundamental such as arts and biology classes. The asynchronous feature of e-mail makes multimedia file exchanges more efficient than when performed using real time applications such as CUSeeMe and Internet Phone, where information is required to be received within a limited time.

With the ongoing developments to upgrade the Internet, by implementing new protocols and technologies to better manage bandwidth and to allow for multimedia transmissions, multimedia e-mail can be a very efficient tool for supporting text based messages, in particular, between students and instructors.

MIME

Multipurpose Internet Multimedia Extensions (MIME) provides Internet users, with different computer systems, with the opportunity to integrate multimedia to e-mail, including graphics, sound, Postscript files, pointers to files and motion video. It also allows them to interchange text in languages with different character sets. Currently not all e-mail clients can handle MIME, but an increasing number of them do.

Videomail

Videomail is another shareware program which adds multimedia to e-mail, and which can significantly enhance electronic mail messages. It allows users to send a quicktime video or audio clip of the sender. The tool digitizes

Figure 1.1: Videomail screen shot
(Source :http:// http://www.shout.net/~dtrinka/home.html)

video or audio, then sends it to the receiver with a Quicktime encoded attachment. Other file types can be also attached to the audio-video messages.

Possibilities and limitations of multimedia e-mail:

Introducing multimedia and audio-video clips is of great value for communication in an educational setting. If used properly, such specifications allow instructors to support their messages with the required multimedia material, graphics, sound or/and video clips, which gives more value to the message, and facilitates the students' assimilation of the class material.

Because of its several advantages, low cost, and the recent upgrades and developments over the Internet, multimedia e-mail is likely to be available and widely used before multimedia real time applications, such as CUSeeMe. Unlike real time tools, the asynchronous nature and time independence of multimedia mail means that sending or receiving a multimedia message does not have to be done within strict time constraints.

Internet service providers are very likely to set their charges based on the amount and speed of delivery of information sent rather than on the connection time. This means that real time applications, which use large amounts of bandwidth and require fast distribution, may become very expensive. They may become a costly option for students, instructors and educational institutions with limited budgets. Multimedia e-mail, on the other hand, will be much less costly.

Some of the main issues of multimedia e-mail include the following:

• Like any other e-mail application, security is a major issue for multimedia e-mail. In order to secure their messages, users will have to use the Privacy Enhanced E-mail (PEM), and its derivatives, a topic which will discussed in more detail in Chapter 8.
• Another issue is that files containing audio, video and graphics use a lot of bandwidth and take time when downloaded. Receiving large multimedia files can easily congest the users network.
• If multimedia e-mail is to be used as a basic means of on-line interaction, the asynchronous nature of multimedia e-mail, time consuming downloads and the possible congestion problems can be very frustrating and inefficient, especially for telelearning users. This tool, in fact, is most appropriate to be used as a support tool to real time text based conferencing where the instructor can send multimedia files and share them with students.

The World Wide Web

Often referred to simply as the Web, the World Wide Web is a wide area hypermedia information service that allows computer users to quickly and easily navigate and access the large information databases of the Internet. The Web can be regarded as the information in the databases plus the links among them. The Internet is the means of communications by which users access these databases. One powerful aspect of the web is its use of hypertext links, which allow users to jump from one file to another. Another important feature, is its ability to support images as well as many other file types, which can be viewed with external viewer programs, including hypermedia documents containing sound and motion video.

The Web was developed in 1990 at the European Center for Nuclear Research (CERN), as a way for scientists to share documents. By 1995 it was the fastest-growing service and the most popular and effective means of information interchange on the Internet. At present, the Web is being used mainly as an information resource, but numerous additional applications are possible.

The WWW is a client-server hypertext based information retrieval tool. A web server consists of software and computer hardware, responsible of sending documents to other client computers when asked to. When a user asks for a document, the client, also called the browser, requests the document from the server. The server responds by sending the text and any other media within that text (pictures, sounds or movies).

In order to be able to send and receive hypermedia files, servers and clients communicate using the HyperText Transmission Protocol (HTTP). Files are written using the HyperText Markup Language (HTML), which is a simple markup language for logical document layout. Logical document layout means defining elements as headings, texts, paragraph returns, lists, bullets, etc. The HTML file contains links to other information sources identified by its Uniform Resource Locator (URL) which is essentially its address on the Web.

Many commercial Web browsers are available today and many are based on the NCSA Mosaic design, which is one of the original browsers. Most of them include new reading capabilities, menu maintenance tools for bookmarks and extensive sound card support. New versions are more efficient and more powerful, as they contain many new extensions, including virtual reality and 3D-object manipulation, audio and video, and languages such as Java and

ActiveX, which run independent of which operating system is being used.

Because of the large volume of information on the web, security is very critical. Encryption and authentication methods allow sending and receiving secure data and selection as to which clients receive information. This allows freer and more secure communication among Internet users, and ensures privacy and protection of information.

The WWW today is a very basic element in educational environments, at all levels. As mentioned above, the WWW grants several educational opportunities for students, by providing them with access to a wide range of knowledge. Using the web, students not only can learn information from others, but also gain ideas by looking at their peers' reports and experiences. This also stimulates them to be more active in contributing than if they were in a traditional classroom, passively receiving material. It also empowers them to move from local to global discussions. Using the WWW also provides them with an easy touch to "high-tech" experience, which significantly increases their motivation to take part in on-line environments.

Commercial software is available for the Web, providing features specifically tailored to the needs of telelearning. Examples include:
- Virtual-U (http://virtual-u.cs.sfu.ca/vuweb/) from Virtual Learning Environments Inc.
- WebCT (http://www.webct.com/) developed at the University of British Columbia
- Mentys (http://www.globalknowledge.com/) from Global Knowledge Network
- Pebblesoft (http://www.pebblesoft.com/)

The features offered by telelearning Web-based software are useful to students, instructors and administrators.

Student-related features typically include:

- Communications tools, including asynchronous conferencing among course participants, email to individual course participants and real time "chats" among groups of course participants.
- Course content search tools, including key word searches for image-based content, and searches of glossaries and indexes of course material.
- Grade-related tools, including tests to be performed at specific points in the course, plus self-evaluation multiple choice quizzes that can be performed at any time. Students can also view their own marks compared to the marks for the class as a whole, presented, for instance as a histogram.

• Presentation tools, including a students home page plus an area for making individual or group presentations to the other course participants.

Instructor-related features typically include:

• Content-related tools, including authoring and/or the ability to import content from other software
• Student management tools, including the ability to set up student groups for discussion and project purposes, track individual and group student progress, and identify students who are exceptional in any way.
• Access control tools, allowing students access to for instance a presentation area where they can leave material for other students to view.
• Testing tools, including automatic administering and marking of multiple choice quizzes.

Administrative features include:

• Program organization, including creation and deletion of individual courses plus organization of courses into programs from which students can easily select options.
• Performance monitoring, including monitoring the response time of Web servers, plus statistics related to number of students accessing the system at different times of day.
• Grade management, including receipt of grades from instructors and approval for issuing to students.
• Access control, including granting access privileges to students and instructors.
• On-Line registration, allowing students to register for courses on-line.
• Prerequisite management, including checking that a student has completed the necessary prerequisites before registering for a course.

There are also a number of training management systems which can be used to provide administrative features for an organizations full range of courses from Web-based courses to classroom-based courses, including:

• Saba Software;
• CyberWISE Online from Saratoga Group
• Pathware from Macromedia
• Plateau

- TrainingServer from Syscom
- LOIS from KnowledgeSoft
- Librarian from Asymetrix

Advantages of the Web

The main advantage of the WWW is that information is dynamic. This is a powerful feature for on-line instructors, since it allows them to change and update their material whenever there is a need for it. Students, therefore, are always kept up to date with the most recent changes and news about the lecture material.

The WWW hypertext format is also an important feature. The use of hyperlinks allows students to browse, jump between links, have quick access to relevant material and to perform searches easily.

Writing documents in the Hypertext Markup Language (HTML) is easy, but used to be time consuming. Today, with the development of editor tools, which assist in designing web sites, users can create web pages without having to insert the HTML codes manually. By attempting to emulate a WYSIWYG (What You See Is What You Get) environment for HTML authoring, web page design has become fast and easy. Such tools are of great benefit for instructors with limited time who want to provide their students with comprehensive web pages with relevant references to relevant course material.

An extensive list of these editors is available at: http://www.yahoo.com/computers_and_Internet/Internet/World_Wide_Web/HTML_editors.

A user can easily translate a regular file into HTML format using tools called filters. These are very helpful, especially in case of long documents, such as hypertext books. Hypertext books allow students to jump between chapters and references without the need for downloading and reading the whole book.

A list of filters is available at: http://www.w3.org/hypertext/WWW/Tools/filters.html.

While designing a course web page, or any other hierarchical document, the designer or the instructor, in case of telelearning should be very careful. Convoluted and complex document structures can be confusing for students and other users. Hierarchical design is not always the best way to get to the required material, and direct access might be, in some cases, easier and less time consuming.

An instructor's web page can be designed using the following principles:

- Make the page design easy for navigation, by providing the user with the appropriate links.
- Limit the number of graphics, especially when most of the users have dial up accounts. If the designer needs to use graphics, a convenient option is to use thumbnails that users can select if they want to see full size photos and graphics.
- Design pages in a way which allows users with different browsers to get the necessary information. Some students or other users might not have access to browsers which support all currently available features.
- Use important key words prominently in the home page so that search engines direct users to that page.

One other important feature about the WWW, is its ability to run multimedia applications, and to integrate audio, animated video, graphics, pictures and text. This represents very good support for teachers during on-line lectures and helps them in creating a dynamic learning environment. Downloading such documents, however, is very time consuming and is not always an easy task, as will be explained in the following section.

Problems and Limitations of the Web

One main problem is that for users to fully benefit from the potential of the WWW, they need powerful computers. If the student has an old computer, downloading images, graphics, sound and video clips can be very time consuming. Today, most of the computer systems available in the market are powerful enough to allow the use of the most powerful features of the WWW. These computer systems easily run the WWW clients and browsers. With the increased availability of such computer systems, prices are becoming more and more affordable for students and educational institutions.

Even when using powerful computers, downloading multimedia files, or accessing popular URLs, is in many cases, very time consuming. This is mainly due to the lack of availability of bandwidth over the Internet backbone, limited bandwith on Internet access lines and the heavy load on the Web servers. Even though many educational institutions are upgrading their connections to more powerful links, high bandwidth connections for students working from home are not available in all cities, see Chapter 6.

In order to save the downloading time, users can turn off the images, so that only text is received. Sometimes however, images, sound and animation are very important to understand a document. To play a movie or a sound clip, plug-ins or helper applications are required which do not necessarily conform to standards. In order to provide all students in an on-line course with all the features of the documents used, it is recommended that all the participants use the same browser, plug-ins and helper applications, which is not always an easy requirement to be satisfied.

In addition to the technical problems, there are also some educational problems, which need to be addressed, in order to ensure the effectiveness of the WWW as an educational tool and to increase the reliability of the published material.

While carrying out searches, students can find thousands of links related to their subject. Assessing the value of the published material can be very difficult and misleading, since any Internet user can post documents over the Web. Standards to evaluate the Web material should be therefore developed, in order to guarantee high value information searches, see Chapter 9.

Another problem, is that the WWW provides a dynamic process of updating and modifying materials regularly. Relocation of addresses and sites is very common; active addresses one day might not be available the following week. This can be problematic in many cases where an instructor provides students with important references, which might disappear before the students access them.

As more users recognize these issues as problems, they can then start collaborating in order to provide solutions. For instance, in order to avoid the overwhelming research results, the Altavista search engine has recently included a new feature called Live Topics. This tool helps users refine broad and/or vague queries and analyze the results of their searches, by selecting additional words and eliminating unrelated topics. The refined query results appear in order of relevance and words inside a topic are ordered by frequency of occurrence. The tool is very powerful in helping users save time browsing documents which are in many cases irrelevant to the searched subject, and in getting directly to the right information resources.

Currently, several technological upgrades are being implemented in order to overcome, the bandwidth problems. High speed modems facilitiate the download of graphics, audio and video. As high speed technologies become more ubiquitous, and broad bandwidth applications such as video-conferencing become more mature and effective, real time applications will be increasingly possible over the web.

Many school systems, both K-12 and post secondary, are aggressively moving to take advantage of the world wide web. In Florida for instance, the Florida Information Resource Network, FIRN, a statewide network has been established linking educators throughout the state. The network is being upgraded so that schools throughout the state can take full advantage of the World Wide Web.

Another prototype for using the WWW for telelearning is CyberEd which is a full credit university, offering on-line courses on the Web, through the University of Massachusets Dartmouth Division of Continuing Education. Its main objective is "to create a distance learning environment that rivals the traditional classroom environment in the quality and the content of the learning experience (it) can provide" and "to provide plenty of opportunities for meaningful student-to-faculty and student-to-student interaction". Currently 13 courses are offered, of which only two are non-credit courses. Classes are limited to a size which allows the instructor to effectively interact with all students. The main Internet tools used in the CyberEd environment are the Web and email.

In addition to traditional resources such as textbooks, students also heavily use the extensive on-line Web resources. Class material and assignments are posted on-line in a Web page, with hyperlinks to extra relevant material. Assignments and projects including multimedia files and graphics are submitted on-line via e-mail, and can be later posted on-line for others to consult. Class members' interaction is mainly asynchronous, providing a flexible environment for students with different schedules and needs. Moreover, CyberEd courses also make use of forms, for class interaction and testing.

Currently hundreds of students are taking courses with CyberEd. Its flexible environment, eliminating time and place restrictions and allowing for easy access and reach to valuable information are the main advantages which are encouraging more and more students to join this type of environment.

CyberEd home page is available at: http://www.umassd.edu/cybered/whatis.html

Web Conferencing

The continuous developments of the Web, coupled with the increased need for real time interaction in a user friendly environment, have encouraged developers to make use of this medium to hold conferences, such as on-line chats or on-line lectures.

in the form of Usenet newsgroups. When support for forms input was added to HTML, conferencing over the Web became possible. Web conferencing is a form of web-based group discussion that uses web browsers and servers to provide users with an interactive medium.

Figure 1.2 is an example window in web conferencing software which consists manly of a form where messages to threads are added as well as options of reading previous messages within the same thread and other threads, a help and a main page button.

Within a telelearning environment, applications of web conferencing are very effective in creating a dynamic learning environment. One interesting application of this tool, is to hold on-line class discussions, and to support messages with hypertext links to Web resources. As a result, students can have a better understanding of the lecture material and class time is used more efficiently as discussions can be held for a longer time. Moreover, links to previously discussed topics can significantly reduce the need for lengthy quotes from previous messages.

One of the main reasons for using Web conferencing over the Internet is that the Web offers a large number of client and server software which support a wide variety of hardware. Proprietary systems are very unlikely to match the Web's universality. The main strength of the Web is that it provides a common user interface for several utilities such as FTP, or File Transfer Protocol, Gopher and WAIS, or Wide Areas Information Service. Extending

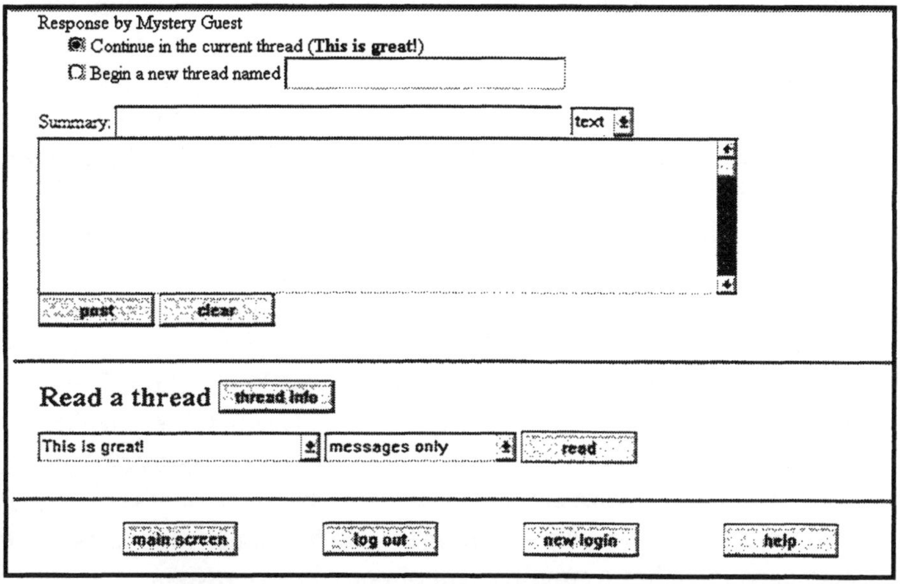

Figure 1.2: Sample of a web conferencing form
(Source http://www.emaze.com/cgi-bin/cgiwrap/emaze/demo)

the Web's service to conferencing, allows users to have access to the Internet's invaluable resources and to interact with multiple parties, without leaving the familiar environment of the Web, and to interact with two or more people. Furthermore, a conferencing system on the Web can be designed to scale well. As the data can be distributed across any number of servers, there are no inherent limits to growth.

A Web conferencing tool is usually a normal http server with added capabilities. This server keeps track of all users located on pages, serves for a public chat area and relays the data in the public conferences to the participants. Private conversations and public conferences are handled differently, to minimize the load on the server. For private conversations, the server simply provides the two parties with each other's address, the connection is made directly between the two. For multiparty conferences, the user sends the message to the server, which relays it to other participants. Messages are received with data identifying the sender and the discussion it was sent to, since some web conferencing tools allow the user to be involved in several conferences at the same time.

A comprehensive list of web-conferencing tools and resources available at : http://freenet.msp.mn.us/~drwool/webconf.html#freeware as well as at: http://www.yahoo.com/Computers_and_Internet/Internet/ World_Wide_Web/Chat/.

There are several features and powerful characteristics of web conferencing tools, which make them far superior to mailing lists and listservs. These features can be summarized under the following points:

1. They allow for separate conferences for several subject areas. The common feature of all Web conferencing tools is that they provide a basic level of organization. In addition on focusing on different subject areas, different conferences have different social rules and etiquette to follow during discussions. For an on-line course, this feature would be useful for groupwork, where one student can be involved in more than one discussion group each with a different subject area.
2. They provide users with threaded discussions within conference, which is a good way for organizing information. Threads sometimes take the form of a tree structure, where each topic is the main root for branching responses. This structure however is not always convenient since it makes discussions fragmented. One solution to such problems is the star structure, where each topic has a simple chain of consecutive responses attached to it. Users can easily understand this form which closely resembles real life

conversations. WebNotes and HotWired's threads are examples of web based chat areas which use the star structure.

For on-line students, this feature allows them to keep track of the discussions even when they are not on-line. Even though most of the discussions are held on-line, the option of adding responses at any time, adds value to class discussions.

3. They provide users with a list of topics in a conference. In addition to the list of topics, many web-conferencing tools indicate the amount of activity in the topic, such as the number of responses and the date of the last response. Such information is also sortable both by topic start dates and by last response dates.

4. They respect the integrity of topics by allowing users to go back to the start of the beginning of the topic and to follow it all the way through to the most recent response. This allows students to refresh their information and to better keep track of the conversation, especially if the discussion was held during lecture time, and where the instructor had important points and comments. In order to avoid clutter, the instructor can filter out discussions and keep only the relevant material.

5. They provide users with the ability to perform searches by date, author and keywords on both topic titles and message texts.

6. They furnish the options of holding private and public conferences. Some web conferencing tools require a conference host or moderator, who is usually the instructor, for an on-line class. The moderator usually has flexible control over the discussion and has the authority to limit access to the desired participants. Some tools give some participants read and write permission, others read only and others no access. This is very useful for holding on-line lectures and for private group work. It is the moderator's responsibility also to manage the discussions and to keep discussion on track

Issues and Challenges

There are more than 60 web conferencing systems today, compared with just two at the beginning of 1995. Although Web conferencing is always improving, it is still easier for heavy users of interactive tools, such as on-line students, to telnet to a simple text based real time conferencing tool such as MUDs and MOOs. The problem, however, lies in the Web architecture itself and not in that of the Web conferencing systems.

The first problem is performance: the Web is very slow for highly interactive applications because of the overhead involved when navigating large amounts of material. Delays when choosing links can significantly hamper smooth communication, especially when participants are trying to interact in a nearly synchronous way, during a group or class discussion for instance.

A second major problem is user interface. Navigating a Web conference is performed using the embedded HTML links. The lack of key board navigation can further slow down browsing messages. Web software developers are currently working on solutions to this problem by incorporating HTML frames and Javascript.

Another problem is that with the existing web conferencing tools, users have to always write messages into forms. Upgrading the tools to support uploading of existing files would save more time and make real time conversations faster.

Web conferencing tools are asynchronous. Even though they are designed to emulate real time chat, it requires input from the user to update a web page resulting in a time lag.

Another issue, is the lack of users' support. Only a few of web conferencing tools today, have "wizards" that guide users through the installation and the interaction process, while many others do not.

Next, even though web conferencing tools enable users to include sound files, animation and still images in messages, this can pose problems. Including a link to an already available image on a web server is no problem. Adding a new image to the server however is difficult. The user should be able to import the image from a drawing program, type a message and send it. This however requires both more sophisticated HTML document editors than the ones available today, as well as coordination between the web server, the web client and the document editor. The new HTTP-NG (Next generation), the updated version of hypertext Transfer protocol promises several improvements in performance and in coordination of server/client connections.

Including HTML links in messages might interfere with the functioning of the conferencing software and might be disorienting for users. Extra formatting of the display should be applied in order to distinguish between message content and structural elements of the web conferencing tool, which is a difficult design issue.

Involving active links in messages might disorient the conversations as students might start browsing the web during discussions. It would be interesting if it is possible to find ways of deactivating links during a conversation and to limit the activated hypertext links during the discussion to a few specific applications.

Another important issue is security. Many web conferencing tools do not provide protection of the delivered material. Others are password protected and therefore restrict access to desired participants only. The security issue is common to most of the Internet tools. Developments and upgrades in this field are continuous and, hopefully, soon most of the web conferencing tools will provide their users with a secure environment.

Finally, bandwidth is the common issue for highly interactive applications. If users do not have high bandwidth connections, interactions can be easily slowed down and impeded, especially when downloading hypermedia files. Some browsers us a faster Web client technology for downloading files: it displays each page as it is being received and aborts transmission if the user selects another link.

Fortunately, many of these problems are on their way to being solved. A new version of HTTP, called HTTP New Generation, or HTTP-NG, will be used in communication between browsers and servers. Under HTTP, the Web browser must establish a new connection with the server for every requested document, leading to time-consuming handshaking procedures. Under HTTP-NG, a browser can maintain an open session with the server while it requests multiple documents. Interaction therefore can be faster. This change, however, will take a while, until software changes to both browsers and servers are made. The independent platform Java applications are also promising many for Web conferencing systems. One main advantage, is that Java based Web conferencing systems can take full control of the screen layout and implement any type of key or mouse interactions. This feature as a result can solve many of the user interface problems.

Netscape is also planning for solutions to offer Internet users with a problem free conferencing environment. Netscape is working on enabling a web site that runs the Netscape server to easily configure their server to host group discussions. It is also trying to upgrade its browser to include a sophisticated built in conferencing interface.

The following is a description of a web conferencing tool called Dialogue which is being used to deliver an Elgin Community College Visual Basic on-line course via the Internet.

The software is used for class discussions and for asking questions about the class material. A Dialogue icon is available for students on the instructor's web page. By clicking on that icon, students can access the Dialogue discussion area, see all related questions that have already been asked, as well as the instructor's replies. Students can ask follow-up or new questions. By having all the previously asked questions posted, students and the instructor save the time of repeating the same question and answers, and provides student with timely answers.

One important feature of this tool is flexibility: Users have total control of the messages that are posted through Dialogue. With an administrative password, they can edit or delete any message, and they can rearrange messages into more logical discussion areas or categories. When viewing and responding to messages, a user has the option of highlighting or viewing only the most recent messages. Replies can be viewed by discussion category, or as a whole set.

Based on the Dialogue users' experience, this tool allowed a diverse group of students with different needs and life commitments, to talk and interact together. With each lesson having its own discussion area, students can split into groups and have their own discussion in a separate area.

Dialogue is available at: http://www.mcs.net/~pelczars/magic/dialogue.htm.

Future developments

Several developments are taking place over the Web in order to improve its use and its educational value and to make it more suitable for live interaction. The following section describes some of the main current developments, which are relevant for Telelearning. They include: HTML upgrades, Hyper-G, Adobe Acrobat, JAVA and VRML.

HTML upgrades
HTML is continually evolving and upgrading providing the Internet community with more powerful features. Examples of advanced features are:

- The inclusion of tables using a markup style suitable for interpretation on wide range of output devices, including Braille and speech synthesizers.
- Catering for non graphical browsers. Text can be flowed around figures and the user can control when to break the flow to begin a new element. Including this feature makes the WWW more convenient for many students with different browsers, and helps reducing the download time since, they might not need all kind of viewers and applications for some documents.

- Support for equations and formulae, compatible with most word processing software, using a simple style of markup. This feature increases convenience for math students in writing their documents and avoids the drawbacks of having to convert math to on-line images.
- A static banner area, present at all times while the student is surfing the Web. This area can include disclaimers, notes, warnings, class announcements, and customized navigation and search controls.
- Support on forms for graphical selection menus, scribble on images, file upload and audio file.

All these features provide the instructor as well as the student with rich opportunities to improve on-line interaction while benefiting from the rich Web resources.

Hyper -G

Hyper-G is an information system, developed at Graz University of Technology, Austria, created as an alternative to the WWW to overcome problems of finding information while searching the web. The WWW was actually designed for smaller amounts of data and as it grows the searching problem increases. Hyper-G, as its developers describe it, is a WWW system for significant amounts of information. The main difference between the WWW and Hyper-G is its structuring facilities. In Hyper-G documents are grouped in clusters, which can be grouped in collections, which can be also elements of other collections. The advantages of such hierarchy are very important. First, navigation and data administration is much easier. Also, automatic CD ROM production becomes possible and, finally, much link editing disappears.

Hyper-G is fully compatible with current Internet technology and includes seamless access to popular Internet server technologies such as WWW and Gopher. It provides for hyperlink consistency to and from multimedia documents, full text retrieval, and client gateways to Gopher and World Wide Web browsers. It also supports real multimedia tools for structuring, maintaining and serving heterogeneous multimedia data including text, images, digital audio and video, PostScript and 3D scenes.

The main advantages of Hyper-G over the WWW as summarized by Maurer, one of Hyper-G developers, are:

- Hyper-G's new hierarchical system, significantly eases data administration and provides better support for users. This therefore opens up new possibilities for users especially in educational environments where information search is very basic.

• It is capable of handling a variety of data types including animation and 3D (VRML).
• It has multilingual support .
• It provides a powerful, hierarchical scheme of access permissions.
• It enables a user to add private links to documents they don't own.

Java

Java is a full featured object oriented programming language similar to C++, which lets developers create small applications called applets, that run on any kind of computer. Its main advantage is its platform independence, which allows users to execute programs on the server. Java's architecture was designed to allow for efficient multi-platform operation on the Web or internal network, while minimizing maintenance time and development costs. Java's applications or applets reside on the network in centralized servers. The applet is delivered to the user's system whenever it is needed, and starts running immediately.

Because of the user-friendly environment the Java applets provide, such as animation and 3D manipulation, Java-based web conferencing systems are becoming more popular. Using this tool in telelearning, will provide users with a quicker, easier and more dynamic learning environment, which consequently improves their assimilation of the material and allows lower school levels to apply telelearning.

Adobe Acrobat

Adobe Acrobat is a software package which enables users to exchange and view fully formatted documents, with advanced features like text with different typefaces, multimedia, graphics and photographs, regardless of platform, operating system or application used to create the originals. Recipients later can navigate, annotate, print or store the received document. This tool has further expanded the capabilities of the Web.

Preserving the original feel of documents is very important in an on-line educational environment. Using this software, instructors can convert electronic files created using different applications into the Adobe Portable Document Format (PDF) and publish them on their Web site for students' use. Instructors therefore can guarantee that their files will be seen exactly as they want them to be seen. This, therefore, not only improves the quality of the delivered material but also saves delivery time and money.

The Acrobat Reader home page is avilable at: http://www.adobe.com/prodindex/acrobat/main.htm.

Acrobat has several features, which provide students with convenient methods to navigate and manipulate data in the document. These features include:

- Compressed file sizes, which therefore saves the download time, and increases the efficiency of lecture time, if files are sent during a class session.
- The ability to change, select, copy and paste text from the document into other applications. Students therefore can capture and use information for their own personal use, such as other reports and assignments.
- The ability to annotate a document, customize it with a personal label and to merge notes from multiple sources into a single Adobe Portable Document Format (PDF) file for further review, or to summarize all the other students' and instructors' annotations in a single complete file.
- Key word searches throughout the whole document. This enables students to perform quicker searches, even in illustrations, charts and tables of documents indexed with Acrobat Catalog.
- Links and bookmarks allow the user to move between files.
- Enables zooming, which allows users to magnify the page and therefore better view the page in more detail; especially useful in biology and photography courses.
- Users can password-protect PDF files, and can also enable or disable printing, changing the document, adding and changing notes, and selecting text and graphics. This is a very useful feature for instructors in case of sending copyrighted materials or if a document should not be changed, such as medical images.
- Adobe Acrobat files can be faxed or printed in color or black and white, at any resolution.

VRML

The Virtual Reality Modeling Language (VRML) is a language for describing multi-participant interactive environments via the Internet, hyperlinked with the world wide web. Such environments allow users to rotate 3D graphics, which provide users, and mainly students, with a better simulation of objects. This tool is used in several educational courses, including medicine. Integrating VRML in on-line classes provides students with a better understanding of the displayed objects than the 2D graphics, and better simulates reality. Some problems still remain to be resolved such as the slowness of downloading 3D files, and the high CPU requirements of 3D displays.

Chapter 2

■

Real Time Conferencing Tools

Text-based Conferencing Tools

The following sections describe the three main real time text based conferencing tools over the Internet, which are the Internet Relay Chat or IRC, the Multi-User Dimensions or MUDs and the MUD Object Oriented or MOO. Based on these tools, several customized environments have been created. An extensive list of these environments is avilable at: *http://www.itp.berkeley.edu/~thorne/MOO.html.*

We first describe each tool, as well as some applications to the telelearning environment. This is followed by an analysis of the advantages and limitations of these tools.

Internet Relay Chat

The IRC is a worldwide on-line conferencing system, which allows real time text based conversations among multiple users.

An important feature of IRC is the channels. Because it is a networked service, IRC can have thousands of people talking at the same time organized into different channels. Each channel can be thought of as a room devoted to a particular topic or a group of people. These channels are very suitable for virtual classrooms or group discussions, where every group of students of a particular class can have their discussions separately. Participants in different channels can move from one channel to another, and send mail to other people in other channels.

One other main feature is that sessions of the IRC can be recorded for further reference, which is particularly useful for on-line class discussions and lectures.

To join the IRC, a user uses a client program called irc to be connected to an IRC server. Each IRC server is linked to other servers in a large web of data exchanges. The servers manage the complexity of tracking users, channels and messages. Once connection is established the server is responsible of relaying all the commands and the messages to the network and vice versa.

Because of the universal access to IRC and the large number of users, risks of inappropriate behavior are very high. In order to prevent this, users who create channels become channel operators. In addition to owning and running a channel, a Channel Operator (Chan-OP) has complete control over the channel, including making the channel private, limiting access, and making the necessary restrictions to avoid any offensive behavior.

Users can also get assistance from the IRC operators. Their primary responsibility is to maintain servers and to eliminate problems with IRC connections in general.

One main problem with IRC is that communication is done by typing, which for many people impedes smooth communications.

Within a telelearning environment, IRC represents a very efficient tool to support the on-line course delivery. After browsing the class material, students and their instructor can meet on a regular basis on an IRC channel and hold class discussions and ask questions about the materials they have already studied. The instructor can act as the Chan-OP by monitoring and controlling the flow of discussion. IRC channels can also be used for holding smaller group discussions within a class session, and to work on group projects.

MUD: Multi User Dimensions, Multi User Domains, Multi User Dialogue or Multi User Dungeons

MUDs are text based multi-participant virtual environments accessible via the Internet which allow users from different places to interact in real time.

MUDs evolved out of multi-player adventure style games in the early 80's. Later MUDs began to evolve into more social and educational areas for discussions, instruction, information exchange, and lead to the creation of elaborate, networked environments.

These virtual environments usually comprise thousands of interlocked descriptions of various settings and rooms. These can be linked to other rooms forming a house, an educational institution such as a campus, or any other organization, and from there to a virtual town, city, forest or whatever the creator's imagination desires. These environments were found to be very suitable for establishing a telelearning environment, and are being heavily used for this purpose. Several virtual institutions are a simulation of the "tangible" university or college building, while others are completely virtual areas, which have been constructed by the designers out of their imagination. A virtual campus, (or any other educational institution), usually comprises an information desk, to answer students' inquiries about subscription and other information, an administration office for dealing with subscription and all other administrative issues, virtual classrooms, where students meet with their instructions and hold class discussions. Instructors also have virtual offices where they can "meet" with their students, and answer their questions, and finally a student lounge where students can socialize and chat about different subjects. Several other extensions can be added to virtual institutions. Some are reproductions of the tangible institutions.

Technical aspects

The original idea of the MUD has evolved over the years using the client/ server architecture. The main features of a MUD server are:

• To manipulate the database of objects in the virtual world, the current players' names, descriptions and state (active, inactive), rooms, rules and other miscellaneous features of the MUD.
• To allow the extension of the set of objects.
• And to accept network connections from clients.

The clients' software is usually written in the C language. Telnet is one such client program, which allow users to connect to MUD software. The client's primary task is to send and receive input/output between the server and the user. The MUD server exists on one machine, while the client is typically run by users from their machines. Many clients today are being upgraded and developed with different features in order to improve the user's communication. Some of these features are filtering users output by separating the different outputs in separate lines and providing users with macros to execute several commands with just a few key strokes.

There are many types of MUDs available on the Internet. They vary in many details, such as their embedded programming language, and their storage methods for the objects they manipulate, as well as in theme and interests. All of them, however, have the capacity to allow multi-party real time communication.

Once connected, users on the MUD are provided with a brief description of the MUD, its purpose as well as other instructions about how to get help about using different commands, such as those used for communication, movement, paging etc. Several MUD sites also provide their first time users with behavior guidelines in order to keep a suitable environment for discussions.

The concept of text based environments is very flexible, as users can move freely between the different rooms using easy commands, and creating hundreds of environments with different themes and interests.

The main features of MUDs therefore can be summarized as follows:

- They are interactive in real time where all participants can exchange messages immediately. This feature provides on-line students with conditions similar to face to face classes, where spontaneity is the main characteristic of such discussions.
- A MUD environment enables users to make meetings as private or as public as they want. This is very useful for on-line campuses, where classes can be easily separated from other campus areas. Also this facilitates real-time group discussions and group work.
- A MUD environment enables MUD-mail for personal messages and bulletin boards and mailing lists to create interactive environments.
- MUDs are multi-user capable allowing thousands of users to communicate and exchange information together. This feature allows students to exchange ideas in real time with experts and other students around the world, which enriches discussions and moves discussions beyond the class limits.
- MUDs allow users to download multimedia files, allowing the instructor to better simulate face to face classes and to support their lectures by the necessary graphics, audio and motion video. This therefore allows many more subjects to be taught on-line, such as biology, architecture, music and arts.
- MUDs sessions can be recorded for further use. Thus for an educational institution, for instance, students can retrieve previous class sessions and discussions for reference. Clients are also capable to save transcripts of files providing users with a permanent archive for their use.

MOO: MUD Object Oriented

MOO stands for Multi User Dimensions-Object Oriented. As its name indicates, a MOO is a variant of a MUD but it includes more possibilities for interaction between MOOers. MOOs, like MUDs are virtual reality sites allowing users from different locations to log into a virtual room and communicate and conduct discussions in real time. Users are able to move from one room to another, talk, page and mail people in other rooms. The MOO database consists of a basic set of programs and functions. All other operations rely upon these functions and programs to operate.

Unlike MUDs, MOOs allow users to build, interact with and manipulate cyber objects (including furniture, pets, and imaginary objects), make additions to the landscape, in addition to chatting with other people. In fact it is a programming interface which allows users to freely manipulate and extend the environment by creating their own objects.

A MOO can be used as a conferencing system for on-line lectures. Versions of lectures and messages can be accessed later by students and teachers whenever they want. A MOO therefore can be used as both an asynchronous and synchronous environment.

In a MOO there are different user levels. The highest level is that of a wizard. The wizard is a moderator, who is in most cases the instructor or a system operator helping the instructor. The wizard has to build, or program the MOO which can be time consuming for many instructors.

The powerful features of MOO's have resulted in the creation of very flexible environments, which are proving to be of assistance to educational institutions. MOOs provide a metaphor of real life by allowing users to interact with objects as they would do in real life, and allows the simulation of real environments. The Virtual On-Line University and the Diversity University have designed their own MOO for delivering courses. Other institutions and instructors are also moving more and more towards MOO as a means of augmenting their classes.

Virtual objects such as a virtual slide projector allows the instructor to show every student on-line a series of slides. These slides are basically short paragraphs of prepared text that the instructor prepares to emphasize specific points. Another virtual tool is the virtual video recorder that tapes the conversations going on into the classrooms and storing them in a virtual tape library. Tapes of each session can later be retrieved by students whenever needed. Some professors have even designed virtual theaters for students presentations, video cameras and TVs and a conversational robot acting as

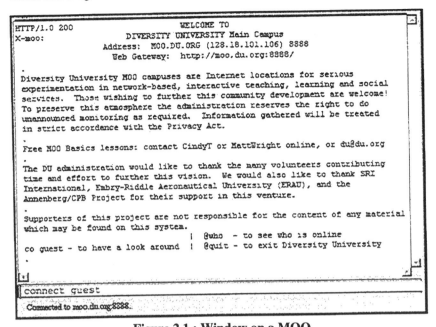

Figure 2.1 : Window on a MOO
Source: http://www.du.org/java/CupOmud/snapshots/

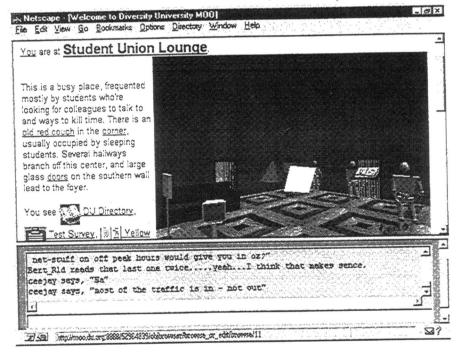

Figure 2.2: Web interface of a MOO with the integration of VRML
Source: http://www.du.org/java/CupOmud/snapshots/

vocabulary tester, tutor, room guide, and information assistant.

Most MOOs have a basic theme around which the are developed and built. Diversity University, for example, is an educational MOO, so the building and development has been that of a college with many administration offices, classrooms, a student union, student lounge as well as other areas such as those found in a real campus.

Figures 2.1 and 2.2 demonstrate a window on a MOO, and a MOO web interface with VRML integration.

Advantages of Text Based Conferencing Internet Tools

Text based conferencing systems are very suitable for telelearning environments via the Internet. The increasing number of on-line courses offered using these tools confirms this idea. It is mainly their synchronous characteristic that is contributing to their popularity. Being able to interact in real time significantly promotes the flow of information interchange between class members. Text based conferencing provide the telelearning community via the Internet with several other conveniences, which are stated under the following points:

- Text based conferencing tools' low bandwidth and low cost requirements enable students from around the world to have access to on-line classes, especially those unable to use traditional methods of delivery.
- The real time feature of these tools and the ability to access web resources provides virtual areas for students and researchers to share information and to make quick referrals to relevant material. This powerful feature can significantly improve the effectiveness of an on-line course and improve the learning process.
- MOOs are most appropriate for same time different place communication. Therefore it is appropriate for telelearning and on-line courses, where it is desirable to have the class together for interaction.
- MUDs, MOOs and IRCs allow for immediate responses and quick question-and-answer sessions, a very necessary and useful feature for on-line telelearning. For distance education, a student at home can connect to a campus computer, telnet to a MOO site and join his fellow classmates in synchronous discussions.
- Because responses are immediate, these environments are more revealing of the students' reactions to the received material and discussions, knowledge and behavior. Such tools therefore can be very useful for remote

testing.
- Real time communication allows students to interact and collaborate easily. Students can work in groups on-line, which improves distance communication and saves time as opposed to group work using asynchronous tools such as e-mail.
- Group work held on-line takes place in separate rooms and synchronous discussions can take place in conditions similar to face to face classes.
- MUDs and MOOs can be configured in a wide variety of ways and provide users with a very flexible interactive environment. Users can perform any form of interaction including talking to objects, looking at bulletin boards, participating in discussions, and walking around. This flexibility however comes at a cost: MUD environment design is very time consuming.

Common issues with text based conferencing Internet tools

Text based conferencing software used over the Internet have also some limitations, such as:

- Even though most of the systems are able to accommodate many participants, a classroom full of about 300 students having a conversation all at once would be chaotic. In case of on-line classes, it would be better to limit the number of students in a class, according on the instructor's group management skills. These environments, however, can be very useful for group work, where the number of participants is small.
- User training is very important in these environments, in order to allow them to make use of the system at its full potential. While the set of commands required to effectively use MUDs and MOOs are limited in number, users need practice and instruction before using them, especially when dealing with young students. One significant weakness of some MOOs is that its commands always use the @ character. Something that a user can easily forget during their chat. The IRC also presents some similar difficulties where users are required to precede their commands with /. New IRC clients, today are making their environment more user friendly by allowing users to use buttons instead of characters. User training, however, is still very important and essential, to ensure smooth and effective chat environments.
- For many users, the fact of communicating by typing impedes smooth communication.
- It can be disorienting. Text based conferencing tools consist of reading lines of text and then typing fast enough before it scrolls away. Communication

therefore may degenerate into a competition as to who can type faster or better.

• Typing is time consuming and cannot always express what a user is thinking.
• Also, many users cannot express themselves properly by just typing their thoughts, and find that visual interaction is as important as verbal interaction.
• Talking with people you don't see might be frustrating for some users.
• Having multiparty discussions can cause some interaction problems such as the domination of the discussion by some members.

These problems require a well skilled discussion moderator to mediate and to monitor discussions, who can be the instructor in case of on-line classes. These skills, however, are not easily acquired, and need a lot of training and effort.

• Learning to administer a MUD is very difficult and time consuming. This involves making sure the database is backed up and learning the MUD's programming language in order to extend the environment.

Technical issues

In order to run text base conferencing software a server is required. The operating system is also important. Most MUDs and IRCs run on UNIX or Linux software.

Connection speed is also an important factor to consider. With the recent developments and broadband features such as Virtual Reality, downloads of graphics and audio and video clips, students may need high speed Internet access.

Despite all these issues, the increasing popularity of these tools for delivering on-line courses prove their usefulness in telelearning environments. The continuous developments and upgrades, such as the integration of Java programming language which enables embedding WWW pages, and the more friendly interface designs have made these tools more convenient for on-line students and instructors.

Text-Based Conferencing in Practice

One case example is the Diversity University. According to its developers, Diversity University was the first MOO to be designed for classroom use. It is a non profit on-line instructional organization, with the main objective of increasing the availability and access to knowledge to people all around the world and to meet the different telelearning needs of people and individuals.

DU's mission statement as reported by its board is:

> The mission of Diversity University is to develop, support and maintain creative and innovative environments and tools for teaching, learning and research through the Internet and other distributed computing systems, and to guide and educate people in the use of these and other tools, to foster collaboration in a synergistic climate, and to explore and utilize applications of emerging technology to these ends in a manner friendly to people who are disabled, geographically isolated or technologically limited.

The primary medium used by DU users is the MOO environment. DU has three main active MOOs: DU-Main MOO, DU-South MOO and DU-Press MOO. DU-Main MOO is the only open site for public access. It is designed as a campus, with several buildings such a student lounge, an administration, a gym and a football field as well as different faculty departments. Within each building, several educational projects are included which were created by the DU community and that can be used as part of a class or for simple on-line discussions. DU-South is a Research and Development MOO where programmers can meet for collaborative research, train, experiment and create.

DU visitors can access the DU MOO either using the telnet program to access DU using text only, or using a web window for a multimedia communication.

Thousands of students, teachers, and administrators worldwide, today, are using DU classes, literature, and consulting services. The medium's easy access coupled with the potential benefits it offers to the educational community are the main reasons for its increased popularity.

DU's Home page address is: http://www.du.org/index.html.

Audio-Conferencing Tools

Because text based conferencing tools are time consuming, many Internet users are using audio-conferencing tools. Instead of spending the time writing, students can use their time watching, listening and talking, which is somewhat similar to a traditional face to face lecture.

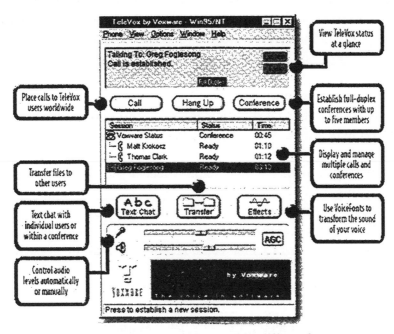

Figure 2.3: TeleVox window and its diffrent features
Source: http://magenta.com/cyberphone/teleweb1.gif

Good quality audio in an audio-conference is very necessary. Humans are intolerant to audio delays, especially when it comes with video and is unsynchronized with the video stream. In three studies conducted by Tang, John C. et al. noticeable audio delay in video conferencing made it difficult for the participants to manage their interactions. They also showed that users prefer having audio with minimal delay over having audio in sync with video if a noticeable delay is imposed.

Audio-conferencing tools present a major potential for Internet users, including educational institutions. One of their main advantages is that they are cost effective, low bandwidth and low cost. Much of the audio-conferencing software is available for users for free and requires only basic hardware. All that a user needs is a PC or a Mac running Windows or OS/2, a microphone, a SLIP or PPP net connection, and a modem or a LAN connection. Since most programs compress the voice message, low bandwidth connections are in many cases enough to receive acceptable voice quality.

Some of the widely used audio tools are: Netphone, SpeekFreely, Symposium, Learn.Everywhere and TeleVox. Figure 2.3 is an illustration of the TeleVox audio-conferencing tool and its features.

Web based audio conferencing tools offer comprehensive collaboration capabilities suited to a structured group environment. Some systems integrate hardware and software to incorporate regular telephony in addition to audio over the Internet. In addition to audio conferencing, features available include:

- Application Sharing in which an application can be either viewed by other participants and/or the other participants can gain control of the application.
- Shared Whiteboard allowing multiple users to display and annotate information
- Web Browsing, allowing an instructor to access and display live Web sites to participants
- Video streaming for viewing pre-recorded video clips
- Student Testing for real time on line evaluation of student performance
- Text-Based Discussions which can be recorded for archival purposes

Advantages of Audio-Conferencing Tools

Some audio-conferencing software, such as Internet phone run on top of some text based conferencing tools such as IRC, providing users with a list of listeners, and topics discussed. In an on-line class setting, this feature allows instructors to better manage their lecture and to use their time more efficiently. Oral discussions can be, for instance, used during regular class times, while textual communication, can be used during tests and exams.

Some audio tools incorporate "Avatars" to represent the users in a virtual environment. An Avatar is a 3 dimensional human like character that can move around the environment and meet other Avatars representing other users. Audio conversations take place among groups of Avatars. High school students, representing themselves as Avatars, have participated in collaborative projects in urban planning and architecture, to build a city in a virtual environment. Proponents of Avatars believe they have several advantages over the use of live video to represent the user. First, video can pick up busy background in the users office or home such as untidy bookcases, which counteracts the usefulness of seeing the person. Second, good quality video requires high bandwidth Internet access, which is not available to all users.

Issues with Audio-Conferencing Tools

One main issue with audio-conferencing tools, is the lack of compatibility of the different audio-conferencing software. In many cases participants in an audio-conference can only communicate if they are using the same audio-conferencing software. Others can communicate with software, which uses the same standard protocols for audio coding and transport.

The new RTP (Real Time Protocol) is presenting new opportunities for Internet audio-conferencing users. RTP is standard protocol, which is being used by the audio-conferencing tool Vat, as will be explained later. RTP is emerging as a new protocol which can provide interoperability to the different audio-conferencing tools which currently can't talk to one another.

Another problem, is that many of the available audio-conferencing tools are half duplex. This means that participants should wait until the other party finishes speaking to be able to speak. If used in telelearning, this feature can cause several conversation problems. For instance students will be able to ask questions or to comment only after the instructor finishes his explanation. Group and class conversations can also become more formal since communication cannot be interactive.

Many audio tools, such as Internet Phone, are being upgraded today to include full-duplex capabilities so that both participants can speak at the same time. In case of an on-line class, the instructor's role is to manage and organize conversations.

Video-Conferencing Tools

Video-conferencing technology is another important resource, which is predicted to be an important element of a networked online educational environment. Using video in support to audio and text based interactions adds value to a conference and significantly enhances communication. Participants can see each other's gestures, facial expressions, and in many cases assimilate the lecture material better, especially for classes where visual support is necessary, such as arts and photography classes.

Using the traditional methods of video, costs of equipment, telecommunications and special purpose videoconferencing rooms, are in many cases prohibitive. These costs and the time consuming preparations for a video-conference, have limited the use of video-conferencing, especially when it comes to educational institutions with limited budgets.

Several products, such as RealAudio, Xing, and VDOnet, have been released to deliver real-time audio or video. Users, however, have been experiencing several problems with these kinds of tools for a variety of reasons. Many tools are proprietary, and not standards-based, a discouraging factor for using them in a telelearning environment. Using non standards-based tools means that all conference participants should be using the same tool in order to interact. This requirement is very difficult to satisfy in a telelearning environment, especially when students are scattered all over the world and are having access to different tools. Moreover, the unicasting network delivery mechanism used consumes huge amounts of bandwidth and server CPU cycles. This significantly increases delivery costs, and lowers the efficiency of real time transmissions, especially for a telelearning environment where time lags are intolerable, and video and sound quality can be very critical.

The need for better video quality and wider access to more participants and students, has encouraged the development of new low cost video-conferencing software for use over the Internet. Two main tools will be discussed under this section: (i) Reflector-based conferencing, which is the first video-conferencing software over the Internet, operating within a unicasting environment and (ii) The Multicast Backbone, the Mbone, which is being more and more integrated in the Internet environment, to provide high quality and effective video-conferences over the Internet using multicasting.

Internet video-conferencing has many powerful aspects, which can be used effectively in a telelearning environment. Instructors at any time can communicate with their colleagues on campus or throughout the world, to consult, exchange ideas or to teach. Collaborative learning between students and several classes is also very important and possible using the new Internet tools. Virtual office hours are possible, allowing a more immediate and interactive communication than e-mail or text based conferencing.

Real time visual interaction makes conversations more effective, by allowing participants and especially students, who might never meet face-to-face, to see their classmates plus nonverbal language such as gestures and expressions, very important cues in an real time interaction.

Many Internet users today have performed live video-conferences over the Internet, despite the network's limitations, such as low bandwidth and lack of support to real time applications.

Recent standards such as IP Multicast, Resource ReSerVation Protocol (RSVP), Real Time Protocol (RTP), as well as continuous upgrades for compression techniques of existing video-conferencing tools will soon make video-conferencing a common application over the Internet.

Reflector-Based Conferencing

An example of reflector-based conferencing is CUSeeMe, an Internet based multimedia conferencing platform, developed at Cornell Information

Technology (Cornell University, Ithaca, New York), to provide the Internet community with inexpensive multipoint computer conferencing. CUSeeMe was the first software for the Internet that allowed multiparty video-conferencing. Recent versions of CUSeeMe enable viewing up to 8 participant windows, and allow for an unlimited number for audio and talk windows.

Since its appearance in 1992, CUSeeMe has dramatically evolved. Its primary applications have been telelearning, graduate supervision, and research collaboration.

Figure 2.4 shows a CUSeeMe video-conference snapshot.

How it works

Reflector-based conferencing consists of a client program and a server-like component called a reflector. Conferencing applications require continuous bandwidth and have different requirements from a packet data transmission protocol. Technologies such as World Wide Web browsing and file transfer utilities use a connection-based method like the TCP protocol and need packet confirmation and loss control. The audio and video streams in multimedia conferencing use UDP, the User Datagram Protocol instead, which gives priority to new data over correcting errors in what was previously

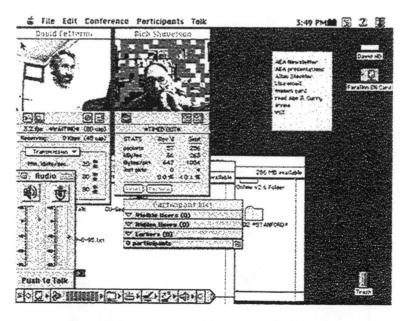

Figure 2.4: A view of a CUSeeme video-conference
Source: ftp://gated/cornell.edu/pub/video/html/fetterman.html

sent.

The server, known as a reflector, allows conference clients to have all types of group communication (one-to-many, and many-to-many), depending on the users needs and hardware capability. The reflector is responsible for routing multiple streams of video, audio and text during a conference and reflecting them to all participants concurrently. Without reflectors only point-to-point links connecting two users are possible.

Reflectors act as intelligent multicast stations providing conference and network management tools for the instructor. Conferences can be configured to be private with password protection, restricted to bandwidth usage, defined to allow users to connect for the required time. This feature is very important when holding small class discussions or on-line oral exams where presence is restricted to class members. For very large conferences, reflectors can be chained together, allowing more attendees to participate. Chaining also helps distributing the network load over a number of subnets within a WAN. This method can also be very helpful in a telelearning environment, especially when students need to meet with their counterparts from other areas around the world to work on common projects.

As shown in Figure 2.5, the reflector takes one CUSeeMe video input stream from the source, makes multiple copies for each user who wants to receive the video stream, then sends them to the appropriate destinations. The same is done for audio and data streams. Not all sites receive all streams. For instance some sites may be capable of audio and data but not video. Running a reflector therefore, requires a large amount of processing power and bandwidth, since multiple copies to every connected participant should be made.

Reflectors are also very helpful in managing bandwidth. When network traffic is heavy and packet loss of individual users is running too high, the reflector can adjust the transmission rates. For example, when the first person

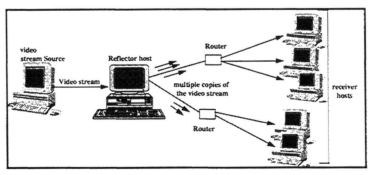

Figure 2.5: Reflector operation

is speaking, the related audio is prioritized (followed by the video), over the other conference attendees. Also, the data for supporting applications like whiteboard and file sharing are managed by reflectors.

Each participant can decide to be a sender, a receiver or both. Reflector-based conferencing software provides three major types of information transport: audio, video and auxiliary data.

Receiving video requires only a personal computer with a video board. Some Reflector-based conferencing software such as CUSeeMe can be downloaded for free from www.cornell.edu.

Sending a video stream requires the same tools required for receiving video, in addition to a camera, such as a small, low cost, digital camera that can be mounted on the top of the computer monitor, and a video capture board.

Once connection is established a video image of each participant appears on the computer screen. Digital video images may be captured from a camcorder or a similar inexpensive video source fed into a digitizer and then compressed by the software. Video compression software sends only changes to the image, so that a still background is not repeatedly transmitted. Although acceptable video images are possible with 28.8Kbps modems, a five person video-conference requires five times the bandwidth at the reflector.

Audio information is captured using a microphone and sound card on the computer. A good quality microphone is desirable. Audio packets are compressed and transmitted directly to the other connected parties either on a push-to-talk (using a mouse button) or a "squelch" (when sound is high enough) basis.

Auxiliary data is another feature in reflector-based conferencing, including textual chats, whiteboard plus annotations, high resolution images and file sharing. These features have proved to be very important for classes in medicine and other subjects where the material has a high degree of visual content.

Advantages of Reflector-based conferencing

Using reflector-based conferencing for holding on-line lectures and discussions can be very beneficial for creating a dynamic learning environment.

First, reflector-based conferencing brings multimedia conferencing to a wide user community by making it compatible with all the major desktop computer platforms. Earlier conferencing software was oriented to powerful workstations not generally available to primary and secondary schools, or residential Internet users. Reflector-based conferencing has opened multiple party video-conferencing to users of low end desktop computers, and has enabled a broader participation in the desktop video technology.

Second, it is built on an open technology, the Internet, and standards based transmission protocols. This means that students and users from anywhere in the world can use it as long as they have an Internet access and the required hardware and software.

Third, the original version of CUSeeMe, was distributed as "freeware" from Cornell University at no cost. Current commercial software is sold at a price that is affordable for students, especially when compared with all the features and services it offers. Moreover, the required hardware is very basic and cheap. As a result, students with limited budgets can use the software and benefit from its powerful features for holding real time live video lectures.

Reflector-based conferencing allows for improved bandwidth management, allowing students with limited bandwidth to benefit from the software. It incorporates low bandwidth compression technology, which reduces the amount of bandwidth used. It also offers scaleable compression and decompression "codec" technology, which allows each user to control their own bandwidth usage. For instance, modem users, such as on-line students, can select the codec that offers the best quality for low bandwidth transmission. They can also set minimum transmission rates that will adjust to the variety of network connections they may be using, i.e., ISDN, modem, LAN connection. If network traffic is too heavy for a reliable conference, transmission will remain at the lowest setting and only move up when the network is less congested. For instance, in network conditions where a significant amount of data is lost, CUSeeMe uses packet loss information to automatically adjust the video and audio transmission rates. As packet loss increases, it adjusts the bandwidth by reducing the transmission rate. The audio quality is automatically maintained by prioritizing audio packet transmission over video. Finally, CUSeeMe uses "Forward Error Correction" techniques to recover from audio packet loss; thereby maintaining quality in adverse network conditions.

All these features are very powerful in maintaining smooth connections, avoiding interruptions and guaranteeing continuous transmissions of data during important lectures or on-line exams.

In general, most of the features of reflector-based conferencing can be of great advantage in a telelearning environment and help support an effective delivery of on-line lectures. The following features are particularly important:

- Ability to support multi-platforms this includes: Windows 95, Windows 98, Macintosh and Power Macintosh.
- In addition to viewing multiple participant video windows, a user can have a large number for audio and talk windows. Therefore if some students do not support video, e.g. do not have a video camera, they can still take part in the on-line discussions by sending audio and text data.
- Whiteboard for collaboration during conferences, which is very helpful for on-line presentations where the instructor needs to display slides and make annotations during a lecture. Also, students can use it during on-line group discussions for brainstorming and collaborative work.
- File sharing capability, including two modes of operation, where a participant in a conference can display a file for other participants (a) allowing them to view the file, (b) allowing them to edit and make copies of the file. This is very useful for group projects in which students can be jointly developing a shared document.
- Direct launch from Web pages, which is a very powerful feature enabling class members to have flexible access conferencing through Web pages.
- Phone Book which allows saving, adding and editing participant addresses and reflector sites which can be very useful for the instructor, as well as to students, to keep a record of each other's references.
- Security: in addition to the passwords and caller ID, other conference and inbound call security are also provided.
- Local window controls for microphone, video, status bar, and connection information.
- Picture Adjust Slidebar to control brightness and contrast.

Issues with reflector-based conferencing

Security is an issue for reflector-based conferencing, since anyone who connects with an active reflector can view the ongoing conferences. One way of handling this problem is a caller ID feature, which pops in a message alert box informing participants of incoming connections. System administrators who manage reflectors can also help providing a level of security, by configuring the reflector to accept a specific list of IP addresses, such as registered students. The system administrator can further restrict remote access to the reflector by adding password protection. Therefore, it is only those who possess a password can access the reflector site and attend the ongoing conferences. As more system administrators upgrade their reflectors to include these options, better controlled multi-party conferencing environments are produced. For a point to point conference, privacy and security of the transmitted data will always be dependent on the security settings of the users' networks and that of the Internet as a whole.

In many cases, communication between sites may not be completely fluid. Because of delays, each person needs to signal when they finish speaking. These delays can be disturbing during on-line lectures where continuous sound is required. Moreover, humans are less tolerant to audio lags than to video lags.

Another drawback, which can also apply to any video-conferencing tool over the Internet, is that on-line video-conferencing is more invasive than other on-line communications such as audio and text based tools. On-line users can easily forget that they are on display, forgetting to be attentive about their behavior.

Bandwidth is another important point of great concern for individual users, especially for students using simple 28.8 Kbps modems. During a video-conference, each window open on the user's work area consumes a portion of the bandwidth. In order to reduce the bandwidth consumption, it is therefore important to monitor the number of opened windows. This can be done either by simply closing some of the windows or stopping the reception of those video streams. Setting transmission and receive caps also help to conserve bandwidth. The problem, though, is when the user doesn't have an idea about the appropriate transmission and reception rates which should be set. On-line assistance in this case is required in order to guide users to make the best use of the tool.

Telelearning experience with multimedia conferencing
Despite these issues, the powerful features of reflector-based conferencing is encouraging more people in the educational community to adopt it for delivering education. Many institutions have been experimenting with it for some of their courses and will soon be using it as a basic element for class discussions and communication. Also, several instructors are using it for course delivery and to communicate with their students.

The following are two case examples where CUSeeMe has been used for holding on-line lectures.

Students from different parts of the world, taking the undergraduate Cognitive Psychology course with the Virtual Summer School (VSS) for Open University in United Kingdom, attend their class on-line, using their computers and the CUSeeMe software. Students participate in class discussions and attend guest lectures transmitted from other universities.

David Fetterman, from Stanford University, introduced CUSeeMe to his ethnography class students and used it in the classroom, between other class rooms and to facilitate communication. When he was away from campus, the instructor was able to hold real time live office hours with his students. The new interactive medium enabled him to maintain all his campus schedule of duties and appointments and to avoid time lost to travel. According to Fetterman, "...Internet video-conferencing (has been) enhancing (the class members') educational experience, allowing a more immediate, more interactive form of contact than e-mail." He finds that electronic communication becomes more personal and a lot more effective when tone nuances are heard and nonverbal language such as gestures and facial expressions are seen. The tool was also used during multi-site research projects with other instructors. Participants shared research results, maps and, illustrations instantaneously. This experiment, according to Fetterman, can have considerable implications for international research and cooperation. Fetterman also used the tool to give on-line workshops for students in remote classes.

Despite the several technical problems encountered during his experience, Fetterman's conclusion was that, once the technology and the tool become more mature, the educational community can fully benefit from the potential advantages of CUSeeMe. Using this tool can significantly enhance exchange and expand instructors' reach and accessibility worldwide. As a result, international collegial communication and research can be enhanced, opening new applications and opportunities for educational exploration.

The MBONE

Introducing the MBONE

The MBONE stands for the Multicast backBONE of the Internet. It is a virtual network constructed on top of the existing Internet, consisting of hosts and routers connected to the Internet and communicating using IP multicast.

The MBONE facilitates live interaction and large scale distribution of multimedia material, including live audio, video and exchanges of slides, files, and sharing any other digital information.

These features, coupled with the universal reach of the Internet, is making the MBONE an exciting possibility for the Internet, to move a major step beyond its current mainstream applications, transforming the Net into a universal live multimedia medium.

Evolution

The MBONE originated from the Internet Engineering Task Force

(IETF) experiments in an effort to multicast audio and video over the Internet. The first audio transmission of a conference over the Internet took place during the Spring 1992 IETF conference in San Diego, while the first video transmission took place during the next IETF conference in Boston.

Since then, the MBONE has undergone a phenomenal growth across the world and is deployed and used in all the continents. The Internet multicast technology is deployed today in the Internet infrastructure in routers and desktop operating systems and applications. To date, the MBONE has been primarily used over the Internet for conducting multiparty video-conferences. Some, but not all, ISPs support the handling of multicast IP packets. As more networks are upgraded to support multicasting, the MBONE and the Internet will eventually become a single entity.

An advantage of the Mbone for telelearning students scattered in different parts of the world is that Internet multicasting is a standard, which was developed and tested by the Internet engineering community.

Even though it is quite easy today to create, manage, distribute and access multimedia material using the MBONE there are still some problems. An improved Internet infrastructure is required in order to make the MBONE more usable for telelearning. This will be discussed in more detail in the following sections.

Today, the MBONE is mainly used by academic and research institutions. Many trial projects and live research conferences are being held over the MBONE. Many people are employing the technology for collaborative educational projects, medical imaging, data analysis and groupware.

One prototype of MBONE applications for telelearning and collaborative research is NASA's JASON project. The JASON project is an annual, two week expedition to remote areas in the world, which is received by educational and research institutions around the world, including the United States, Canada, Mexico, Australia, as well as many other countries in Europe and Asia. Its goal is to allow students to interact with scientists using state of the art interactive technologies such as the MBONE. An example expedition topic was volcanos in Hawaii. The session was announced on-line in a press release, inviting educational institutions, teachers, students and researchers, who have access to the MBONE to take part in the live session. Using the MBONE, hundreds of thousands of students from around the world were able to participate in the session and interact with the scientists on the site. Students were even able to control ROVs—Remotely Operated Vehicles—from their remote locations.

Successfully realizing such events requires significant planning and

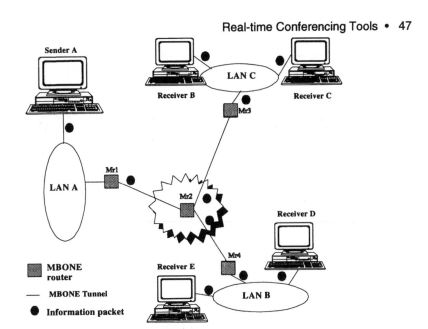

Figure 2.6: Multicast packet path over the MBONE

organization. The MBONE potential benefits for the educational community, however, make these preparations worth the effort.

Multicast

The MBONE consists of a subnet of Internet multicasting routers and end equipment that can interpret multicast IP addresses and can process multicast packets. Other Internet routers and desktop operating systems can only handle and process unicast packets. The MBONE, therefore, is layered on top of the Internet sharing the same physical media. Multicast packets can travel through routers which can only route unicast packets using a scheme called tunneling. Internet routers are continually being upgraded to make them multicast-capable and most major desktop operating systems are able to handle multicasting including UNIX, Windows and Macintosh.

Figure 2.6 provides an overview of the topology of the MBONE and the routing of multicast packets.

As shown in figure 2.6, sender A can send a multicast packet to receivers B, C, D and E in networks C and B, without replicating the information packet. The replication occurs at the MBONE service provider multicast router Mr2. Mr2 makes two copies of the information packet: one for LAN B and a second one for LAN C. Each networks' multicast routers (Mr3 and Mr4 in this case), replicate the received packet to the appropriate receivers.

Without multicast, as shown below in figure 2.7, traditional unicast multiparty communication follows the three following steps:

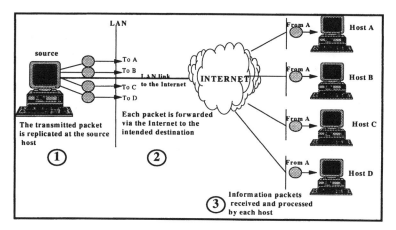

Figure 2.7: Stages of a traditional multiparty communication

1. first the packet is replicated depending on the number of destinations
2. Second the copies are forwarded to each destination.
3. third the packets are processed by each receiving host

As the number of destinations increases, network traffic increases, leading to congestion. This makes the unicast based communication for multiparty communication unsuitable.

Using multicast solves this problem, by eliminating the replication of packets until the latest possible point on the path from source to destination. The host no longer sends the packet to each address of the conference participants. Instead a single copy is sent to the multicast address. This represents a major advantage for network operations, as less data processing is required and lower traffic is transmitted over the intermediate Internet links. This consequently, increases the network efficiency and makes it more suitable for real time applications.

Compared with the MBONE, reflectors using unicast must send multiple copies of each packet, one for each participant in the conference. This causes excess traffic on the access line from the reflector to the Internet and also within the Internet itself.

The multicasting address scheme for group communication started with the work of Steve Deering of Xerox PARC when he developed multicast at the IP level. An Internet addresses with first byte value between 224 and 239 are used for multicast. A small subset of this class (which include the range 224.2.*.*) are reserved for multimedia conferencing.

The multicast addresses are not specific to a particular network interface

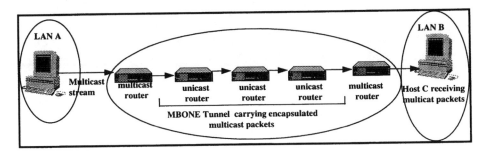

Figure 2.8: Virtual multicast point-to-point link using IP-in-IP encapsulation tunneling

or physical site. They are dynamic, existing only as long as a group of hosts are interested in sending and receiving multicast packets.

Each multicast packet has a TTL (Time To Live) value associated with it. TTL specifies how far a multicast packet should travel and how many mrouters it should cross in order to reach its destination. TTL limits the distribution of a session i.e. from local distribution with a low TTL value to worldwide distribution with a TTL up to 127. Setting the TTL enables an instructor to restrict access to the session, for instance to local students on a university campus. However any student within the TTL range can access the multicast. For private sessions where only specific participants are allowed (e.g. only those remote students who have paid registration fees), encryption must be used.

Tunneling

Tunneling is the scheme which is widely used to forward multicast packets between the islands of MBONE through unicast routers which cannot handle multicast packets This is done by encapsulating, or hiding, the multicast packet into a regular unicast packet. This tunneling method is also called the IP-in-IP encapsulation.

To form a tunnel, a host or a client, sends the multicast packet to the local mrouter. The latter encapsulates the multicast information inside a standard unicast IP packet. This is done by placing the original multicast packet into the payload part of a normal IP packet addressed to the mrouter on the other side of the tunnel, then sending it directly to the intervening routers and subnets. The receiving mrouter at the other end of the tunnel then strips off the encapsulation and multicasts the packet appropriately.

Tunnelling allows portions of the network, which do not support multicast to be used to interconnect portions of the network that do support multicast.

Figure 2.8 illustrates the IP-in-IP encapsulation tunneling method described above. The sender generates multicast IP data packets, with multicast addresses. The packets are then sent over the local network to the mrouter, which encapsulates them in regular IP packets addressed to the mrouter at the end of the tunnel. This destination mrouter extracts the original multicast IP data packets and multicasts them as necessary.

As more and more commercial mrouters and systems able to handle multicasting are available, tunnels will no longer be needed.

MBONE protocols

In addition to the IP multicast protocol, the MBONE uses UDP (User Datagram Protocol), RTP (Real Time Protocol), and IGMP (the Internet Group Management Protocol) protocols, in addition to other encoding and data compression protocols.

All real-time traffic in the MBONE uses User Datagram Protocol (UDP) rather than the usual Transport Control Protocol (TCP). TCP provides a point-to-point connection-oriented reliable byte stream protocol. UDP on the other hand is a transport-level envelope around an IP packet with almost no control. One of the reasons why TCP is not required for audio and video is its reliability and flow control mechanism. Occasional loss of audio or video packets for instance, when using UDP, during an interactive session, are acceptable. The delay of retransmission on the other hand (as when using TCP) is not.

One problem with UDP is that UDP packets may be missequenced, and/or lost when transmitted over the Internet, which can reduce the quality of services to the end user.

On top of UDP and IP multicasting protocols, the MBONE applications use the Real Time Protocol (RTP) developed by The Audio Video Transport Working Group within the IETF. RTP allows real time applications to overcome network latencies in order to achieve continuous playback of audio and video streams. Each RTP packet is stamped with timing and sequencing information, which is used in buffers at the receiving hosts. As a result, participants can still perceive conversations as if they are in real time, while actually a small buffering delay has been introduced in order to synchronize and sequence the arriving packets.

Audio and video compression are used in order to reduce bandwidth requirements over the network. Some of the techniques include the ISO standard, Motion Picture Experts Group (MPEG), and the ITU-T standard H.323. For audio, encoding includes Adaptive Differential Pulse Code Modulation (ADPCM) and Group Speciale Mobile (GSM).

IGMP is the protocol used to inform routers about the other directly attached members of an IP multicast on their subnetworks. An IP host uses IGMP to keep the neighboring multicast routers informed about the multicast groups to which it belongs, by sending group membership updates. When a site wants to join a multicast session it sends an IGMP join message to the multicast group address to become a member of the conference. The nearest mrouter starts replicating packets for the site, which then starts receiving and may also send multicast data. It is only those sites, which expressed an interest (by sending the IGMP join message) which receive any information addressed to that multicast group. This results in very efficient utilization of Internet bandwidth since packets for conference participants are replicated at the mrouter nearest to them.

These packets can be sent through different routing mechanisms. The most popular protocol, which is also a standard is the Distance Vector Multicasting Routing Protocol (DVMRP). The IGMP and DVMRP packets are generated with a TTL of 1; this means that these data packets do not go beyond the local subnetwork.

Applications

The main applications available over the MBONE today, are video and audio conferencing and shared whiteboard. Several software packages with these applications are available over the network including multicast to support multiparty communication.

Conference control tools

Every MBONE session needs to be reserved and announced in order to be sent to interested participants. To do so a conference control tool is required. The following section describes some of these MBONE Rendez-vous tools.

SD: Session Directory

SD is used by MBONE users to reserve and allocate media channels, which can be joined by other users. A typical MBONE session starts with the conference control tool SD (Session Directory) or its newer version SDR. The session directory produces a window showing announcements from all over the Internet. Clicking on a session name gives information about the tools used, as well as its time and date. Each session has a time to live value specified if the organizers wish to restrict the extent to which it is delivered over the Internet.

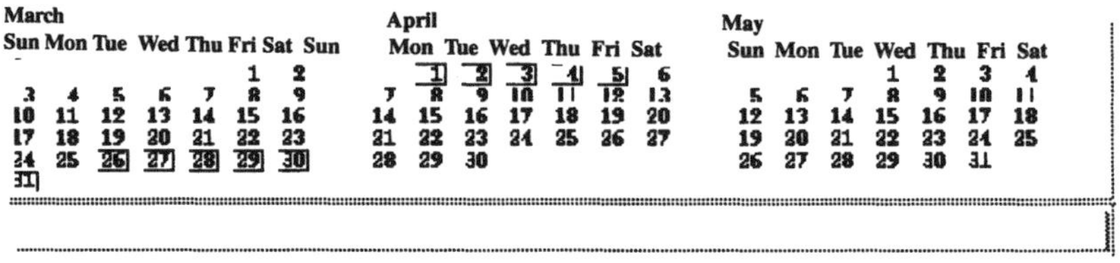

Figure 2.9: SDR calendar window
Source: http://www.cs.ndsu.nodak.edu/~tinguely/mbone-freebsdmbone.html

SD allows users to participate and to create their own session. If a session is chosen, the SD tool immediately launches the associated multimedia applications for the selected session. It can be described as a fully distributed Internet TV guide for creating, reserving and managing the global MBONE multimedia channels or sessions. It's a very sophisticated and powerful package, in terms of its different capabilities for managing and allocating the MBONE multicast addresses among the different sessions.

SDR: Session Directory

SDR is an upgraded version of SD including several more advanced features and functionality than SD. These features include:

- A calendar of the scheduled events for the current and the two following months. This helps users to plan their sessions and to avoid conflicts with other sessions. Figure 2.9 illustrates an SDR calendar. Clicking on a day causes the schedule of that day to be displayed.
- The ability to link to web browsers, and to download files and images from the Web. For a class setting, instructors as well as students can therefore support their material by quickly downloading web files.
- The ability to record events is available in case the user can't be present at the scheduled time. This feature is very helpful for students who miss a class lecture. The user, however, has to plan for plenty of disk space for audio, video and whiteboard data. This is sometimes difficult to predict, since different encoding algorithms may be used.
- SDR also supports text, through an application called Mumble. Using mumble is similar to using IRC except that it uses less bandwidth because of the multicast capability. The main advantage is that, for a class session for instance, students can communicate in real time quietly, without disturbing other groups. This can also save huge amounts of bandwidth in case users decide that video is not required for their interaction.

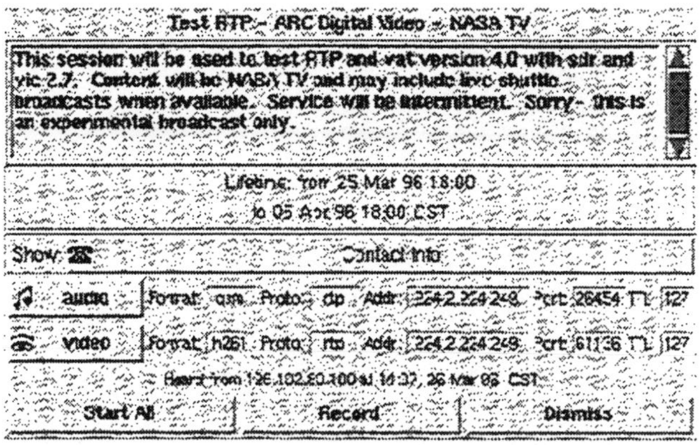

Figure 2.10: The SDR information window
Source: http://www.cs.ndsu.nodak.edu/~tinguely/mbone-freebsd/mbone.html

• Last, and most important, the SDR provides the option of holding a public or private session. If a private session is chosen, it is only those who possess the correct encryption key who are able to join the session. This is very important for telelearning since the course can be restricted to those who have paid the registration fees.

Figure 2.10 illustrates the SDR window with the different information about the chosen session.

MMCC: MultiMedia Conference Control

Multimedia Conference Control, or MMCC, is another session control tool available for MBONE users, which allows multiparty conferencing. Unlike the passive strategy of SD which provides ways for participants to join in, MMCC explicitly invites others to participate in a conference. MMCC allows for confidential sessions by using encryption keys. This feature is very practical and very important for telelearning, where access can be limited only to class members.

Real time Video tools

The Internet is making real time video interaction easy and low cost. Unlike traditional video-conferences, less equipment and bandwidth is required which opens access to the larger community of Internet users, especially on-line distance learners.

The following section describes some of the available software which enable real time delivery of video.

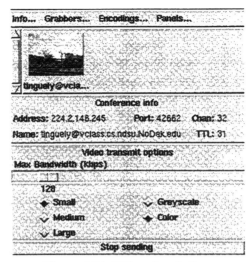

Figure 2.11: NV main window
Source : http://www.cs.ndsu.nodak.edu/~tinguely/mbone-freebsd/mbone.html

NV: network video

NV is the most popular and widely used video conference tool. NV allows participants to send and receive live video over the Internet. NV produces a smooth video texture even during fast moving objects. Like most other MBONE tools, NV can be used for unicast point-to-point connections as well as for multiparty communication. It uses H.323 video coding and also has support for the H.261 video compression standard. It also uses the Real Time Protocol version 1 (RTPv1) to send and receive video streams across the network. Figure 2.11 shows an NV video display with the diffrent tools options.

VIC: VIdeoConference

VIC is also primarily intended for multiparty video-conference, even though it can be run point-to-point. Its main advantage over NV, is that it is able to take up less bandwidth than NV. Much more processing, however is required, and unless a very powerful machine is used, a lower frame rate is produced with VIC than with NV.

Another advantage is that VIC was designed with a flexible and extensible architecture to support the different configurations. It is also based on RTP version 2, which is implemented entirely within VIC and therefore no special system enhancements are required.

One other interesting feature about VIC is its voice-activated switching. This means that a viewing window can be configured to follow the speaker.

Using cues from the audio conferencing tool, VIC switches the viewer window to whichever source is speaking. This feature is very helpful for multiparty communication, such as in on-line lectures, where the video source automatically switched to students who ask questions.

VIC also has a built in data rate control which helps in preventing problems of accidental use of high data rate video feeds.

There are other video tools, which are used for video-conferencing, but most of them are still at their development or experimental stage. Here we have described the most widely used tools.

Real time Audio tools

Audio can be used either as support for a video-conference or as a stand alone means of real time communication. Even when used alone, audio provides important support for real time conversations, since it allows users to express themselves more easily than during textual conversations. Moreover, audio streams do not use as much bandwidth as video. This feature is very important, since, currently, most of the Internet users, including many distance learners, have low bandwidth connections.

The following section describes some of the commonly used real-time audio MBONE tools.

Visual Audio Tool: VAT

VAT is the most commonly used real time audio tool for audio-conferencing over the MBONE. VAT enables both host to host and multihost audio conferencing. It also can use a variety of data compression formats, allowing it to interoperate with several platforms and programs.

Unlike the traditional phone based audio-conference, VAT enables users to view who is speaking by displaying the identity of all those who are tuned in to the session, while highlighting the speaker's identity.

One other main feature of this tool, is the easy archival of audio-conferences into the personal information systems. In case of telelearning, this can be of great help for students, if they need later access to class discussions.

One other important feature is that it provides users with a privacy/secrecy option with password. Access therefore can be limited and data can protected, a very important feature for on-line discussions.

Early versions of this tool, however, had one limitation. It uses half duplex data transmission. This means that only one participant can speak at a time. After finishing speaking, the user should shut off the microphone in

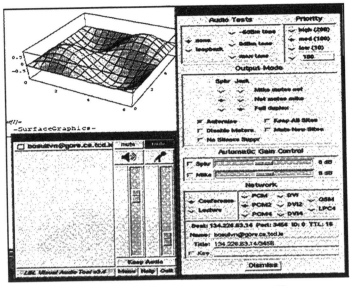

Figure 2.12: Sample session with vat
Source: http://www.serpentine.com/~bos/tech/mbone/apps.html

order to allow other participants to speak. In multiparty conversations, such as during on-line class sessions, interaction could be impeded if a user forgets to shut off his/her microphone. Also, students would have to wait until the instructor finishes speaking in order to be able to ask questions or to give comments. This can limit the efficiency of live interaction where spontaneity and quick comments are valuable.

Upgraded versions of VAT include full duplex capability, where participants use a headset instead of speakers to limit audio feedback.

Network Voice Terminal: NetVot

NetVot is another real time multiparty audio-conferencing tool over the MBONE. NetVot can be used with stand-alone software or in conjunction with the SD tool, for point-to-point or IP multicast-based multipoint conversations. It supports a wide variety of audio protocols. NetVot has very similar features to VAT. NetVot can use either the audio protocol vat or RTP. Using the VAT protocol, allows users to interact with users who may not be using the NetVot tool.

Collaboration tools:

Collaboration tools, as their name indicates, provide support for real time interactions, especially in the case of telelearning, where instructors often need to refer students to course related material, using a whiteboard, or by downloading files. Their main advantage is that most of them are low bandwidth.

Whiteboard

The WB (whiteboard) tool is an example of a low bandwidth MBONE application. The WB tool creates a shared, virtual whiteboard space for conference participants to exchange and share documents, display slides, write comments, draw and type, and is in general used as a visual aid for presentations and brainstorming sessions.

WB allows users also to import slides, which can be viewed by all other participants. WB is a very powerful tool if used in conjunction with real time audio tool. Video is often regarded as unnecessary. It is more important to see the subject matter of discussion on the whiteboard than to see the head and shoulders of the person speaking.

It is important to note that the session control can be loose, meaning that any participant can introduce material into the whiteboard, which increases the risk of unwanted interactions. In order to prevent such problems, sessions can be started in lecture mode where only one user can have control over the session. In case of telelearning, it is the instructor who controls the shared area.

Another main feature is the DES-based encryption which is very helpful in restricting the use of the shared whiteboard to a limited number of persons.

The WB does not use the RTP protocol for transmitting data since it is not as real time as the video and audio communications.

IMage Multicaster Client: IMM

IMM is another example of low bandwidth application. IMM downloads images from the MBONE and displays them. It is built as a client/server based package: the server multicasts graphic images, and the client receives and displays these images on the user's desktop screen.

Shared Mosaic

Shared Mosaic is an extension of the NCSA's WWW Browser Mosaic. Using "What I See Is What You See" collaboration, participants can share a set of URLs at the same time. Sessions are loosely controlled so that anyone can decide to share a URL at any given time. To solve this problem, informal session control via live audio and video tools, such as VAT and NV, can be used during a shared Mosaic sessions.

MBONE VCR

Other tools include MBONE VCR, which is a session recorder and is used to record, playback, and randomly access any MBONE session.

MBONE requirements

The MBONE is a virtual network with routers, which support multicasting. In order to send and receive multicast packets, therefore, a user's local equipment should have the appropriate software for multicast support, plus the appropriate multimedia hardware.

Hardware and software

In order to receive multimedia MBONE events, a multimedia computer with an Internet connection is required, consisting of MBONE software, a color display, an audio/video card, a video camera, a microphone and speakers or a headset.

Sound hardware is available in most UNIX workstations and Macs. For PCs low cost sound hardware such as the Sound Blaster card may be required. To send video, a user needs extra equipment. This includes a video card and a camera in addition to the sound hardware.

For networks lacking mrouters, a workstation can be configured as an mrouter by installing software called mrouted (multicast routing daemon).

Data traffic and network bandwidth

At the time of writing, the allocated bandwidth for the total of all simultaneous MBONE sessions was 500 Kbps. Individual video streams are also limited to 128 Kbps. Many users, however, try to limit their bandwidth by using lower bandwidth audio/video encoding schemes or by limiting their frame rate.

Application traffic

The application data of the MBONE consists of audio, video, graphics, and text files.

Audio: the range of bandwidth required for audio is between 10 and 78 Kbps including packet overhead. The audio applications available over the MBONE implement software compression for reduce data rates. The audio traffic has the highest priority over the other MBONE traffic, because of the low human tolerance to audio delay.

Video: the usual video data rates generated over the MBONE are about

25-128 Kbps. For example, NV produces between 25 Kbps and 120 Kbps at roughly 1-15 frames per second. Video has the lowest priority compared with other MBONE traffic.

Graphics and text: This type of data uses up much less bandwidth than audio and video applications (in the range of 1-20 Kbps.). Peak data rates are achieved when a file is loaded and transmitted for sharing. The rate of interaction during discussions however is only around 1-2 Kbps or less. Graphics and text has a medium priority when transmitted in conjunction with other data traffic.

Network access

For an MBONE session with audio and highly compressed video a Basic Rate ISDN connection allowing 128 Kbps is desirable instead of modem access restricted to 56Kbps. The main advantage of the ISDN is that it offers higher bandwidth.

If the bandwidth of the total event is within the limits of the ISDN line, a user therefore can receive the total event. This is mainly the case of audio-conference with/without the use of collaboration tools such as the whiteboard or the Image Multicaster (IMM) .

Another way to participate in MBONE events, is when the event is provided as many separate events one for video, one for audio and one for whiteboard. The user therefore can select one or more version of the same event to join depending on the connection.

In certain residential and business areas, higher bandwidth Internet access is becoming available including xDSL and cable modems which deliver upwards of 1Mbps to the customer, see Chapters 6 and 7.

For an individual user, such as a student, the hardware and connectivity requirements for using the MBONE are higher than what most of the Internet users currently have. This is why, today, audio-conferences are the most popular interactions. This therefore means that it will still take time until full multimedia live on-line courses can be easily held over the Internet. On-line courses between educational institutions (i.e. not between remote individuals) has been successfully implemented as described under the case study section, Chapter 3.

MBONE feed

If an ISP or an organization wants to join the MBONE, it has to have an MBONE feed. Individual users on the other hand, can have the feed through an MBONE-capable ISP or by direct connection to the Internet.

Issues and opportunities

Bandwidth: Sending multicast data over the Mbone requires the same bandwidth as receiving it, whereas the reflectors used with other conferencing systems require more upstream bandwidth than downstream. This allows the MBONE to be used by customers with ISDN, xDSL, cable modem and T1 access.

• Bandwidth is a scarce resource. Sending simultaneous high-bandwidth video streams, therefore, can easily saturate the network, causing congestion and interruption of the sessions. Moreover, the limit of MBONE traffic today is 500 Kbps, which is not enough for running many simultaneous video-conferences. At full tilt, the MBONE itself can handle no more than four simultaneous video-conferencing sessions or eight audio sessions. As the MBONE user community increases, the 500 Kbps must be increased to handle the increased demand for bandwidth.
• Internet bandwidth is still inadequate in many countries. This would limit the use of the MBONE to only those who have the appropriate bandwidth and only those countries that have installed mrouters or workstations with mrouted software.
• MBONE multimedia conferencing has resulted in an increased demand for bandwidth. This, consequently, is limiting the use of MBONE for real time video-conferencing. Video for telelearning, as disscussed earlier, significantly improves on-line lectures. Limiting the interaction to audio and text based communication therefore limits the efficiency of the medium.

As the Internet backbone is upgraded in capacity it can be expected that more than 500Kbps will be allocated to the Mbone in future.

MBONE management

• There is no central authority to manage the MBONE. It is a self regulatory environment and is loosely managed by the MBONE users community from all over the world in open distributed manner. Any development is therefore a group task performed by several network engineers and developers from all over the world. Preventing actions such as overuse, for instance, by dumping the network with very high bandwidth streams, is unfortunately, very difficult. The fact that no charge is applied for the use of the medium, is likely to encourage increased usage.
• With the increased number of users joining the MBONE, together with the

limited resource environment and the distributed MBONE structure, time management of sessions becomes more difficult and conflicts are more likely to occur.

Misuse of tools

• In case of using half duplex tools, if one user forgets to turn off his/her microphone, other participants will not be able to talk since only one person can talk at a time. Such conflicts and problems are very likely to occur during lectures, where students are used to interrupting the lecture by raising hands and asking questions or speaking out. This can make the on-line lecture less efficient than the traditional lecture. In order to solve this problem extra training and coaching is needed for instructors and students before holding an MBONE conference, until new full duplex tools are developed.

Network issues

• Because of the networked feature of the MBONE, any mistake, such as blasting a high bandwidth video signal over 125 Kbps, can cause network congestion.
• Even though audio broadcast is supposed to be simpler than video broadcasts, preparation of an audio conference is as much time consuming as a video conference, mainly due to eliminating background noise and acoustic feedback from speakers at each participating site.
• As the network becomes more popular, more congestion and higher pressure on popular network time slots can be expected to occur.

Most of these issues are in the progress of being solved as the network is continuously being upgraded and improved.

Other issues

• Even though MBONE users do not pay for using the MBONE, they do not get any guarantees of Quality Of Service (QOS). They currently get what is called best effort service: the system, including the Internet service and the computer desktops of all the participants involved in the session, does the best to always deliver the MBONE service, but with no guarantees for quality.

Mechanisms and infrastructure, today are being put in place, for requesting and reserving bandwidth known as Resource ReSerVation Protocol, RSVP. Also standards known as DiffServe are being developed by the IETF

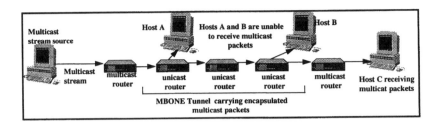

Figure 2.13: Why can some hosts receive multicast packets and others not?

to give priority to some types of Internet traffic over others. DiffServe and RSVP can be used to prioritise audio and video over regular data traffic (e-mail and Web access). In order to limit overuse or misuse of network resources, users may be required to pay based on their use of the network resources and the quality of service rendered by the MBONE.

• Tunneling can be used through non multicast routers to interconnect routers that do support multicast. As illustarted in Figure 2.13, users connected to non-multicast routers, cannot receive the multicast stream.

The increasing developments and network upgrades however, are over-coming this problem, as more multicast routers are being integrated in the network. IP tunneling therefore will decrease and eventually will be elimi-nated leading to more MBONE accessibility.

Advantages of the MBONE for a Telelearning Environment

As discussed so far, the MBONE presents a vast potential for the Internet. The multicasting capability, coupled with the multimedia transmission of time-critical applications over the Internet, supports the increasing conver-gence of visual information and live communication required in telelearning. It has been shown by several studies and experiments that live images and computer desktop-based voice and video conferencing technologies greatly enhances the effectiveness of telelearning collaboration. The free flow of opinions and ideas using voice along with seeing each others' gestures and facial expressions, greatly helps in preserving the human aspect of electronic remote interaction.

The MBONE with IP multicasting is a powerful tool in that it supports multiple party conferencing. The multicast traffic of the MBONE flows over the Internet IP mrouters and then only to hosts interested in receiving the traffic. This Internet-based routing scheme is very suitable for on-line classes since participants can access the session from anywhere.

Another interesting point about the MBONE, is that educational organizations will be able to save on video-conferencing costs and can be able to hold on-line classes, seminars, lectures and meetings remotely, at their convenience and at low cost. Once the software is downloaded, any MBONE user can reserve from their desktop an MBONE channel or session. The MBONE can also be used for secure transmission of multimedia traffic in order to restrict access to only those students who have paid registration fees.

Also the improved bandwidth management and increased capacity of connection lines promise opportunities for the MBONE to become more widely deployed. New technologies may soon provide individuals with T-1 speeds without the expense of an actual T-1 line. ADSL (asymmetrical digital subscriber line) provides Internet access over existing copper lines at a rate of 1.5 - 9.0 megabits per second. Cable modems provide up to 20 Mbps over coaxial cable shared among several subscribers.

Many educational organizations today have Internet access over T1 lines. Therefore, including MBONE traffic does not necessarily require extra capacity. The network traffic, however, should be always controlled and well managed, especially when establishing or participating in an MBONE session, since a busy network can impair the MBONE data flow.

As more protocols are developed, data encoding and compression will become more efficient which further increases the efficiency of using MBONE bandwidth.

According to many distance learning practitioners, the ideal solution would be to combine an MBONE-based distance education course with an on-campus class. The instructor would conduct an interaction-based session, presenting slides and going over web files. During his/her presentation, the teacher would accept questions and discussion from MBONE-connected students as well as in-class students.

Part II
Current Implementations

Part 2 of this book presents a perspective on current implementations of Telelearning via the Internet.

Chapter 3 presents a study of how the Internet is being deployed to support the different administrative and pedagogical functions of virtual and partially virtual educational institutions. Examples of virtual educational institutions operating on-line are included. This chapter is based on a paper by the book authors in the journal "Education at a Distance" (1996).

Chapter 4 provides a summary of the results and the analysis of outcomes of a survey of the on-line educational community. The 10 questions comprised topics about the different aspects of the Internet medium, with the intention of collecting the maximum feedback about current implementations, besides the different impressions of those who have already experimented with an Internet based telelearning environment.

Yahoo! Internet Life magazine held a survey to identify the most wired American schools and to examine how they are deploying the Internet to establish an on-line telelearning environment. A discussion and an analysis of these findings is presented in Chapter 5.

Based on these three chapters, a general conclusion is presented at the end of the section which summarizes all the findings.

Chapter 3

■

Internet Telelearning Applications: Classification and Case Examples

The Internet is currently used for a broad range of educational applications, ranging from accessing reference material to delivering entire courses.

The objective of this chapter is to identify and classify the full range of educational applications of the Internet and to give illustrative case examples of each classification. The classification is then used to analyze trends in the way which the Internet may be used for telelearning in the future.

The classification is divided into two parts:

• A categorization of the methods of teaching and learning over the Internet;
• A categorization of the organizational structure of educational institutions.

Methods of Teaching and Learning

Classification of Teaching/Learning Methods

Delivery of course material
Course material can be organized in the following formats:

• Print, audio and video tapes sent to the student with the initial contact between the student and the institution done through a web site.
• On-line manuals and textbooks hypertext and hypermedia formats.
• Multi-User Dimension Environments (MUDs, MOOs, etc.) where the instructor and the administration staff can have real time communication with the student and provide him/her with the necessary information about the course requirements and administrative procedures.

Class Session

Lecture: The lecture can be either on demand (asynchronous) or real time (synchronous).

Asynchronous lecture is provided through:

• Web pages in hypertext format, with glossaries, indexes, exercises, and references to relevant material on the Internet, or on reserve in the institution's library which could be retrieved remotely.
• Hypermedia lectures and class discussions which could be retrieved when required.

Synchronous lecture can be held using different tools, such as:

• Internet Relay Chat, IRC.
• MUD, MOO environments, which are either only text based or with the option of integrating multimedia files form the web.
• Other conferencing software such as Pueblo and Webchat which allow the incorporation of multimedia (audio and video), 3D scenes and graphics.
• CUSeeMe and Vosaic software which allow for real time audio and video over the Internet
• The emerging MBONE technology which allows multicasting and real time audio and video over the Internet with high quality voice and video.

Class discussions
Real time class discussions are held through any of the following tools:

• Text-based conference software using IRCs, prearranged e-mail sessions, IRCs, MUDs and MOO environments.
• Real time audio and video using CUSeeMe, Vosaic , or the MBONE.
• Listserv, newsgroups and e-mail, especially if students need to discuss subjects with the global Internet community.

Virtual office hours
Support from the instructor can be provided in various ways such as:

• Web page, where students can get quick answers of some frequently asked

questions.
- E-mail: which allows the student to discuss a problem or a question in real time, with the option of integrating relevant material in different formats (text, audio, video, 3D scenes, graphics).
- IRC or MUD sessions which allow the student to discuss a problem or a question in real time, with the option of integrating relevant material in different formats (text, audio, video, 3D scenes, graphics).

Assignments

Because of the ability of downloading and uploading files via the Internet, students are able to send their assignments electronically via e-mail, or using special folders, which can be accessed only by the instructor and the student.

Exams

Students in institutions who take classes with other on-campus students can take their exams in person in an examination center. Some institutions, mainly those which are entirely on-line, allow their students to take their exams via the Internet using real time conferencing software such as IRC, and MUDs.

We now give examples of the above five teaching methods. Many organizations are using the Internet for teaching. The case examples presented here are a selection to illustrate innovative approaches.

Teaching/Learning Methods: Case Examples

Delivery of course material

Virtual-U (http://virtual-u.cs.sfu.ca/vuweb/) is a web-based software system, which allows courses to be offered partially or entirely online. It is being used at 13 locations across Canada involving 3000 students, 50 instructors, delivering credit and non-credit courses in a wide variety of disciplines including English, communications, business administration, computer science, psychiatric nursing, environmental studies, human sexuality, statistics, dance, labour studies, workplace training, Native American languages and education. It is also being used at Aalborg Universitet, Denmark, and University of the West Indies, Jamaica.

At Athabasca University, on-line courses use the Web site as a repository for information about administrative registration procedures and the course study plan. Hypertext student manuals, lists of Internet resources and Internet tools are also provided in hypertext format, which can be consulted when needed.

In a biocomputing course organized by the Virtual School of Natural Sciences (VSNS), a member school affiliated with the Global Network Academy (GNA), 5 authors from USA and Germany prepared a hypertext textbook. The hypertext book contained several links to different databank search services on the Internet. According to the instructors who designed the course, the hypertext book was very effective in integrating Internet resources with the course and in keeping information up to date.

At Indiana University-Purdue University at Indianapolis (IUPUI), students can access reserved material remotely. David Lewis, head of public services for university libraries stresses that Reserves on-line can deliver high quality images, assure document integrity and permitted simultaneous access by an entire class. Moreover he believes that the ability of having a special electronic collection on-line via the Internet, will allow for an efficient and cost effective way of delivering necessary material on demand to several institutions. Students are also provided with references for research resources. These are, primarily, the collections of electronic libraries consisting of course related materials and the cross references provided in hypertext, supplemented by the wealth of on-line information available on the Internet, such as databases, newsgroups, listservs, mailing lists, etc.

Class Session

Lecture
Some institutions, such as
(UND) deliver lecture material to students by mail, and use the Internet for posting summaries, and for real time discussions. Keeping the class sessions on-line, provides students with an extra information resource for future reference.

In a project developed by the Department of Mathematics and the Center for Information Technology Services, both located at the University of Oslo, lectures are designed using the HyperText Markup Language (HTML). Students can navigate freely in the information available, by using different links available in the text. Video-lectures, graphics, exercises, and animated files can also be downloaded. According to many instructors, incorporating multimedia when teaching increases the ability to meet student's needs, and helps to accommodate their life styles and their assimilation rate.

Students from Peter Lalor Secondary collage, in Melbourne, met their counterparts in Singapore over the Internet and performed a range of experiments and discussions using Cornell's multicast reflector CUSeeMe.

The University of Florida and Virginia Tech have used the MBONE to share the expertise of professors between the two institutions. The University of Florida used a conventional classroom with computer projection equipment. Virginia tech used a computer lab in which each student participated in the class using a Sun Workstation. The main advantage of this arrangement was that state of the art graduate topics can be taught by professors who are specialized in that field. Participation of more institutions further enhances this advantage.

The University Of British Columbia uses the MBONE for delivery of 3rd and 4th year undergraduate courses in computer science to community colleges in Kamloops and Kelowna which are several hours drive form the main campus. The perceived advantages of using Internet-based conferencing tools compared to conventional video-conferencing are:

• The software and the communication are almost zero marginal cost.
• There is no need to purchase conventional video-conferencing equipment at the receiving site since computer projection equipment is already installed in any classrooms.
• Existing computer lab headphones for audio can be also used.

PBS has used the Internet multicast capability for a series of live video-conferences for colleges and universities. In addition to the multicast capability, software VDOnet incorporating RSVP, Resource ReSerVation Protocol, allows bandwidth to be reserved across the Internet to ensure jitter-free audio and video.

Class discussions

Many courses on-line are heavily based on group discussions and interaction among the students, especially in the absence of audio and video transmission. This is particularly true of graduate level courses. The role of the instructor, in this case is mainly to monitor the group and to direct and focus the discussion session.

At CyberHigh, a high school operating entirely on-line, students meet via the text based Internet Relay Chat, where they discuss problems and ideas related to the course subject. Because IRC multi-user and multi-channel feature, students can talk in a group as well as on a one to one basis. Usually on-line class sessions are transcribed and made available for further reference by students.

The Diversity University, which is an entirely on-line university, uses a text-based MOO, with the option of adding a web window offering the use of multimedia along with real time discussions. This can be realized by using a browser which supports programs such as Java, which can download to execute multimedia applications.

Some institutions use class listservs and USENET groups, for Internet wide discussions. Professor William, at Illinois State University, who has experimented with these tools in his seminar "Developing and Designing Computer Applications in Arts," states that Internet wide discussions provides valuable input and support for the students, and helps them in solving problems and critiquing their work. Through prearranged e-mails and USENET group discussions, Professor William's students can share the talents and experience of experts, without the limitations of time and geography. After class discussions via synchronous Internet tools allow lengthy discussions and arguments which are not possible in a traditional classroom setting because of time limitations. Moreover, students are found to develop more collaborative and problem solving skills through such discussions.

Virtual office hours

Instructors offering on-line courses also have virtual office hours for students and assistance. After his on-line experiment with 10 on-campus students and 350 offsite subscribers at Pennsylvania University, James O'Donnell stated that he was able to "speak" with each student in his course via the Internet, something that would not have happened if all students were on campus in a lecture hall. E-mail, is judged to be very effective by instructors in providing the opportunity for students to ask questions at any time.

In an experimental on-line course, which was offered at Purdue University, the instructor made himself available at scheduled times for e-mail, on-line talk sessions and conference calls.

As part of its new international "Master's Open and Distance Education" at the Open University, which started in February 1997, students will be using an electronic workbook, which the tutor may ask to see, in which the students record their learning. This allows the tutor to know where students are experiencing difficulties.

Assignments and team projects

Assignments are mostly submitted electronically via e-mail. Students at Illinois State University, taking the course "Designing and Development of Computer Applications in Arts", have private files to submit their assignments, which can be accessed only by the instructor and the file owner. The instructor has also created on-line files where students can share results of their work for critique and discussion. Feedback on an individual basis form the professor can be provided also through e-mail or real time chat sessions via the IRC, MUD or a MOO.

Working on projects in teams is also encouraged via the Internet to encourage interaction, team building and critical thinking among students. The diversity of group members and their backgrounds also adds value to the final work. A team of accounting students from the West Virginia University and Frostburg University has collaborated on a project to solve real world government problems. The team members on each campus designed web pages, where files from both sites were uploaded and downloaded for information.

In some institutions such as IUPUI, students can be asked to write multimedia papers. Through the use of a special system called the Interactive Multimedia System, students can incorporate copy and paste video and audio clips in their papers, save them and use them later for presentations or "hand them in" via e-mail to the instructor.

Professor Knoll of the University of Texas organizes international collaboration among Masters students in MIS, each registered in their own university. Team work involves members from diverse cultural backgrounds, living in different time zones and provides experiences for future careers in virtual organizations in addition to being a means of conducting student projects in MIS.

Exams

The availability of real time conferencing tools, has made the delivery of exams to remote students possible. At Cyber School, students can take exams on-line via an IRC channel. One typical exam is where students are asked one question at a time, similar to oral exams, and are required to answer within a limited time.

The University of North Dakota distance program requires distant students to identify a proctor (a counselor, supervisor, librarian or other responsible individual), who is willing to administer the student examinations.

Organizational Structure

The ability to access valuable information resources and to communicate using synchronous and asynchronous multimedia software brought with it new expectations, needs and demands for a more flexible education. In response to these challenges, new "virtual academic environments" have emerged, taking advantage of the new technologies and addressing one main objective: the timely delivery of high quality, low cost instructional materials to a diverse range of students. These environments include virtual colleges, high schools, universities and on-line classes and programs, which allow people to take courses at their convenience.

These virtual academic environments fall into 3 types of organizational structure, described earlier with case examples.

Classification of organizations

- Campus based institutions offering on-line courses and programs, as an extension to their regular offerings.
- Alliances of campus based colleges and universities, which provide an electronic interface to access different education classes.
- Independent organizations existing entirely on-line which have established their own academic departments and curricula.

Case Examples

Campus based institutions: Space studies distance degree at UND
The University of North Dakota is currently offering a Space Studies master's degree both on campus and via the Internet, with the objective of meeting the needs of students wishing to enter this field or to expand their knowledge, and who have different life commitments that prevent them from attending classes on campus. By taking the course via the Internet, distant students are able to have the same opportunities for discussions and research as on-campus students. Information, links and cross references to other materials pertaining to coursework are accessible on Internet web site. At the start of each term, students receive a package of textbooks, and lecture video tapes. Weekly real time discussions via Internet Relay Chat, are scheduled in order to allow students to discuss and share ideas and ask questions. The

instructor acts as moderator, by controlling the pace of and content of the discussions. Transcripts of previous chat sessions are then kept on-line for students to use for further reference. During the summer, distance learning students attend a two-week workshop, in order to apply and integrate the knowledge acquired during the year.

Alliances of campus based institutions:
California State University Network, CSUNet
    CSUNet is the computer network of the California State University system. CSUNet interconnects California State campuses as well as other "partner" sites like local community colleges, and school district offices within California. The main objective of CSUNet is to a number of other services such as delivery of courses among the "partner" sites.

Institutions existing entirely on-line: Virtual On-line University: VOU
The Virtual On-line University Inc. is a nonprofit organization established and incorporated in 1994 in Missouri with the intent of providing high quality and low cost educational opportunities to a diverse group of geographically dispersed students and to assist traditional and non traditional students in achieving their educational objectives. Currently the VOU is offering 16 courses with transfer credits, taught by professors from six different universities.
    The VOU is operating within a Virtual Education Environment (VEE), which is a Multi-user Object Oriented (MOO) based electronic campus. Students who access the VEE, can have a virtual tour in the university departments office and classes. Instructors have access to any material on the World Wide Web and incorporate multimedia in their class sessions. An instructor can share images and 3D graphics, download video audio clips and give hypertext quizzes and exams, while holding discussions on a text based chat.

Conclusion

Teaching and Learning Trends

    The Internet today is continuously adding advances and developments in the field of distance education. New emerging Internet technologies and powerful tools such as the MBONE, Virtual Reality Modeling Language

(VRML), multimedia languages (such as Java), MUDs, MUSEs and MOO environments, and the World Wide Web itself, allow students in the world-wide community to complete courses electronically without ever having set foot in a classroom.

There are two main trends taking place. The first is the evolution from text based tools (such as IRCs), to off-line multimedia (such as retrieving audio/video files at Web sites), to real time multimedia (such as CUSeeMe and MBONE conferences). Each stage in this evolution requires improved performance from the Internet. As Internet bandwidth is upgraded and technologies such as RSVP are developed to reserve bandwidth, the quality of communication becomes acceptable to an increasingly broad range of educational applications.

The second major trend is the increasing sophistication of the Internet's multicast capability which is essential for educating multiple students. The evolution from USENET groups through reflectors to IP-multicast provides an increasingly flexible and efficient form of multicast for educators.

These trends enable educators to use the Internet not just for delivering course materials, receiving assignments and exams, but also for lectures, class discussions and virtual office hours.

Organizational Trends

An institution like VOU presents a typical prototype of future universities. Its main strength is in the incorporation of emerging technologies, and its ability to accommodate the different needs of a wide and diversified group of students regardless of time and place.

Until recently, close proximity has been a primary consideration for students, and particularly working adults. With the proliferation of on-line courses, location will no longer be the primary criteria for choosing a college program. Instead the course content and organizational flexibility become the deciding factors.

Chapter 4

■

Survey Results and Analysis

Chapter 3 has presented case examples of applications of telelearning by selected major educational institutions. Chapter 4 provides a broader perspective by reporting the results of a survey, which evaluates the use of the Internet tools for education/training by a wide range of educational practitioners.

The Distance Education On-line Symposium mailing list (DEOS-L) provided an appropriate sample of telelearning practitioners via the Internet (mainly instructors and staff members), as well as The Global Network Academy (GNA) instructors. The survey design was patterned after the book *Survey Research Methods* by Babbie (1990) and includes 10 short questions.

The next section provides a description of the survey details, its structure and basic information about respondents. Each of the following sections starts by giving the reasons for asking the question, followed by some hypotheses about the expected results, and conclusions as to whether the hypotheses are validated by the survey responses. Next, the survey results are summarized and are complemented by graphs portraying each set of results. Finally, the conclusion provides an overall summary of all the survey results.

Survey Details

The survey was posted on the 24th of June 1996 on the Distance Education On-line Symposium mailing list (DEOS-L), which is a service provided to the distance education community by the American Center for the Study of Distance Education. This mailing list included about 1423 subscribers as of June 1996.

Another copy of the survey was sent via e-mail to the Global Network Academy president Joseph Chen-Yu Yang, who posted it on the GNA instructors internal mailing list. The GNA mailing list involves about 30 instructors.

The survey included 10 short answer questions: 8 questions with short multiple choice answers, and two questions which requested respondents to write short answers about their personal opinions with regards to using the Internet for telelearning.

The first two questions were asked to get information about the user's function and type of institution. The six following multiple choice questions, investigated the degree of using the Internet, the tools used and any future plans for implementing any extra tools. The two last questions required respondents to give their personal opinions about the advantages and disadvantages of using the Internet within a telelearning environment.

The survey produced 114 responses, where 8 responses were from the GNA mailing list, and the other 106 were from the DEOS-L list. This number of received responses represents a 7.84% response rate. Table 4.1 summarizes these responses:

All replies were received by E-mail. The reply time varied between 24 hours and one month, depending on the availability of the respondent. Most respondents however, responded within a week.

As shown below in Figure 4.1, 53% are faculty members or instructors. The "other" category includes mainly students, educational consultants, assistants, and staff members. The following statistics were obtained from the results of questions 1 and 2.

Nearly two thirds of the respondents' institutions of the telelearning practitioners via the Internet are universities. This reflects that these institutions have easier access to computer facilities than colleges, primary and high schools.

Internet Use for Distance Learning

Interestingly, nearly all the respondents, 91%, were already using the

	Number of mailing list participants	Number of responses	Response rate (%)
GNA mailing list	30	8	26.66%
DEOS-L mailing list	1423	106	7.44%
Total	1453	114	7.84%

Table 4.1: Response rate by mailing list

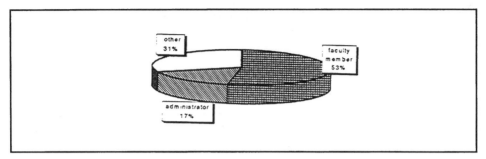

Figure 4.1: Respondents function

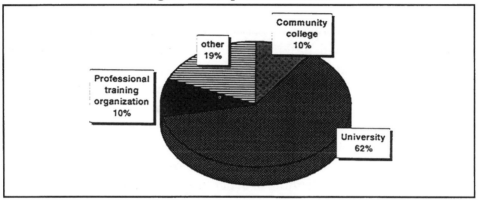

Fig 4.2: Type of institutions (question 2)

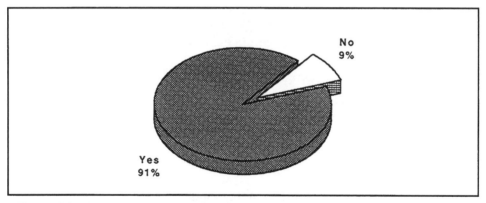

Figure 4.3 : Percentage of respondents who were using the Internet tools in 1995-1996 versus those who didn't (question 3)

Internet in one form or another for telelearning. Among the 10 respondents who did not yet integrate the Internet in their teaching, 8 are planning to use it during the next school year.

Question 5: Reasons For Using The Internet

Background

By asking this question, we wanted to know the reasons that have encouraged telelearning practitioners to integrate the Internet in their courses.

Based on the information obtained while searching about telelearning via the Internet, some of the main reasons of using the Internet for delivering the educational material include:

• Making communication easier between students and instructors.
• Allowing students with different needs to learn in the convenience of their home or office, without wasting time in traveling to campuses.
• Allowing students to take courses and earn degrees on a flexible schedule that is most appropriate and convenient for them.
• Allowing instructors and students to interact remotely with remote experts, and to work with other students form different parts around the world.
• Providing students with a powerful research tool, with extensive amount of valuable information, resulting in better quality and more up-to-date information.

The asynchronous communication nature of various Internet tools, such as the electronic mail, listservs, mailing lists, newsgroups and bulletin boards, is a powerful feature in providing this service.

Moreover, the ability to post, send and access huge information resources at very cheap prices makes the use of the Internet more cost effective than the traditional way of delivering educational and training material.

Survey Results

In order to answer this question, respondents were given seven suggestions, including an other option where they can add any extra reasons. The following results were obtained: 74% of respondents agreed that their main reason for using the Internet is the ability to access and to reach students anywhere and anytime at the convenience of every participant. Another major reason is that the Internet improves communication between the different class members which results in further advantages as will be mentioned in the ninth question.

In addition to the above mentioned reasons, answers included other reasons such as (the number of answers are indicated between parentheses):

- It allows cooperative team learning and creates a more active learning environment. (11)
- It is cost effective since most of the material is on-line. (2)
- It's fun and entertaining! (2)
- It helps students become familiar with Internet tools and technologies.(7)
- It helps students to develop many necessary skills such as writing and discussion skills. (7)
- It is easier to teach Internet classes.(3)
- It is flexible. (8)
- It provides a wealth of information. (3)
- It provides students and instructors with up to date information. (3)
- It is inexorable; therefore, instructors have a professional obligation to make the best learning with it that they possibly can. (1)

A general comment about these answers is that most respondents agreed on most of the suggested reasons for using the Internet.

Figure 4.4 illustrates the responses to each suggested reason

Question 6: Internet Tools And Technologies Used

Background

The Internet offers several tools, some are very widely used such as e-

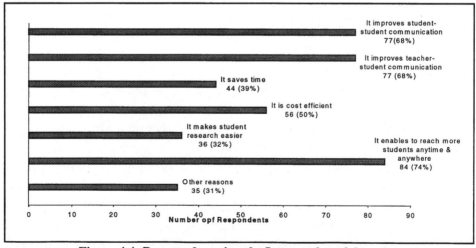

Figure 4.4: Reasons for using the Internet for telelearning

mail and newsgroups, others are less popular such as MOOs and Web conferencing, while others are still at the trial stage and are limited to some experimental sites such CUSeeMe and the MBONE. Because of all these options, we wanted to know what tools respondents were using during 1995-1996 school year, and what tools they were planning to use this year i.e. 1996-1997 school year.

Tools such as e-mail, listservs, mailing lists, newsgroups are widely used by Internet users, especially for instructor/student and student/student asynchronous communication. They are relatively low cost, demand only modest bandwidth on the part of the user. Moreover, most institutions having an Internet access are providing these services to their students, and many professors are finding it very convenient to flexibly communicate with students.

Such tools also allow students to read postings from the instructor or other students at leisure and respond at convenient pace and communicate directly and privately by e-mail with the instructor or any other student. Moreover, newsgroups and mailing lists are in many cases valuable information resources for students when working on research projects. Private mailing lists or listservs, restricted only to class members allow instructors to post their material for students use, saving consequently on paper and other delivery media costs.

Based on these facts, the following hypothesis was formulated for validation later with the respondents' replies:

Hypothesis 1: E-mail and its applications are the most widely used for on-line delivery of lectures and class discussions.

The Internet provides two important low bandwidth tools, which allow real time text based communication. The first tool is the IRC and the second includes a variety of environments depending on the programming language used for interaction. The two commonly used environments are MUDs (Multi User Dimensions) and MOOs (MUD- Object Oriented).

When researching the topic through the Internet, real time conferencing tools, especially MUDs and MOOs, seemed to be increasing in popularity among the educational community. Several institutions have been already using these tools for on-line course delivery. Moreover, the increased developments in this technology are providing users with easier user interfaces and more flexible virtual environments. These two factors can, to a large extent, encourage more institutions and instructors to integrate these tools in their on-line lectures. By comparison, many educators have been using the Web for some time so that there is less opportunity for a growth in Web usage.

Based on the above background information, the following two hypotheses can be formulated :

Hypothesis 2: *The growth rate of adoption of the Internet text based conferencing tools including MUDs, MOOs and IRC is higher than that of the WWW and e-mail applications.*

Hypothesis 3: *The use of MUDs and MOOs within the telelearning environment is expanding at a faster growth rate than IRC.*

In the case of multimedia conferencing tools such as CUSeeMe and the MBONE, the quality of audio and video available over regular modems is limited. These tools are in their infancy with regard to telelearning applications. We can expect to see their usage grow as low cost higher speed modems such as ADSL become more widely available. We therefore formulate hypothesis 4.

Hypothesis 4: *The use of multimedia conferencing for telelearning is:*
a) Growing but
b) Has a lower acceptance rate than text based conferencing tools.

Survey Results

As shown in the graph below, compared with other tools, e-mail is the most popular tool and is used by nearly all the respondents (95%), while the remaining 5% were planning to integrate it during next school year. This confirms the fact it is the tool's affordable costs, in addition to its asynchronous feature and the related benefits, which promoted the quick adoption of the tool within the telelearning community. Since it is almost universally used, its growth rate is lower than any other Internet tool.

E-mail applications, such as newsgroups, mailing lists and listservs, are less prevalent than the elementary e-mail application. Their use however is expanding, with the newsgroups having the highest growth rate. This is presumably, due to the new trend of conferring openly with the larger Internet community, primarily, other students, and experts.

The second most used tool is the World Wide Web, which is already used by 81% of the respondents. The remaining 19% were planning to use integrate it in 1996-1997. For this reason the WWW growth is the second lowest after, e-mail.

Many of the Web's benefits and capabilities, such as its accessibility, its considerable information resources, and its flexible hyperlinked environment, are definitely the main justifications behind its wide acceptance. This rationale is also confirmed by the answers of question 5, where 50% of the respondents consider using the Internet as cost effective, and 32% are of the opinion that that it makes student research easier.

These results partially confirm hypothesis one, since e-mail is indeed the most common tool in the telelearning environment, except that it is the WWW and not the other e-mail applications, which is nearly as predominant as e-mail within the telelearning environment, as illustrated in the chart in Figure 4.5.

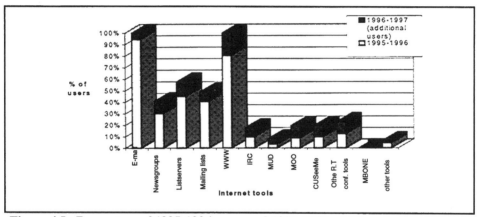

Figure 4.5 : Percentage of 1995-1996 users and 1996-1997 additional users for each Internet tool

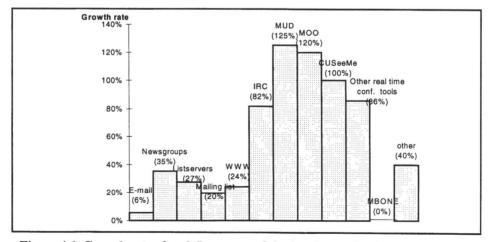

Figure 4.6: Growth rate of each Internet tool during the academic year 1996-1997

As delineated in the chart of the number of respondents (Fig 4.6), those who have already integrated text based conferencing tools is unexpectedly very low (only 4% are using MUDs, 9% are using MOOs and 11% are using IRC). On the other hand, these applications have the highest growth rate during 1996-1997, with MUDs and MOOs having a higher adoption rate than IRC. (125% and 120 % for MUDs and MOOs respectively, versus 82 % for IRC). These results approve hypothesis 2:

Unlike the Web and e-mail applications, which are widely used by the respondents and are nearly at a saturation stage where growth rate is very slow, the three text based conferencing tools are still at the early stages of their adoption and are rapidly increasing in popularity.

The fact that MUD has the highest growth rate can be explained by its more flexible environment than that of the IRC, and its easier programming language than the one used for MOOs. Even though, MUDs are less complex to program than MOOs, the difference in growth rates is not significant (only 5%). This is primarily because of the upgraded and simpler programming languages developed for constructing MOO environments, as well as the more dynamic and flexible MOO environments, which are worth the programming effort. These results agree with the research findings and confirm hypothesis 3:

The use of MUDs and MOOs within the telelearning environment is expanding at a faster growth rate than IRC.

The real time video-conferencing software CUSeeMe has been used by 10% of the respondents, and will experience a 100% growth rate during the 1996-1997 academic year. On the other hand, the growth rate of CUSeeMe is lower than that of MUDs and MOOs (100% versus 125% for MUDs and 120% for MOOs). All these rates are higher than that of the IRCs. The last figure can be justified by the telelearning practitioners' tendency to using the more flexible and dynamic MUDs and MOOs, than the plain text based chat provided by the IRC. These results confirm hypothesis 4, excepting IRC in the text based tools category:

Remarkably, the other real time text based tools, which are primarily proprietary tools, will be having a comparable growth rate to that of IRC. When looking at the detailed results of the survey, those who are using these tools, such as POWWOW and FirstClass, are basically professional institutions, with trainees affording these tools.

As anticipated, the MBONE is not used by any of our respondents, and many of them did not even hear about the technology yet. These findings prove hypothesis 4.

Question 7: Audio and Video Use

Background

Most of the audio and video delivered over the net is on demand. Multimedia clips are downloaded by instructors and students and can be used in class discussions or as further references for student research and assignments.

Because of its lower requirements of bandwidth and low cost compared with real time video, real time audio is more popular than real time video. The fact that most audio tools are proprietary however, and due to the lack of standards, only a small portion of respondents is anticipated to be integrating the tool within their educational environment.

Real time video on the other hand, as discussed earlier under the section of question 6, is still limited to experimental applications and many users are experiencing many technical problems with them. Based on these information, the following hypothesis is established:

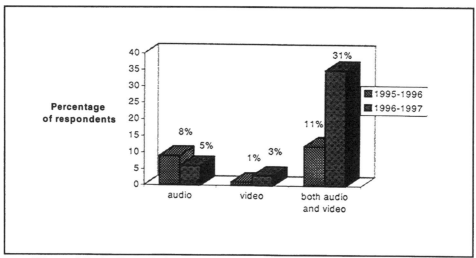

Figure 4.7: Audio and video application for the academic years 1995-1996 and 1996-1997

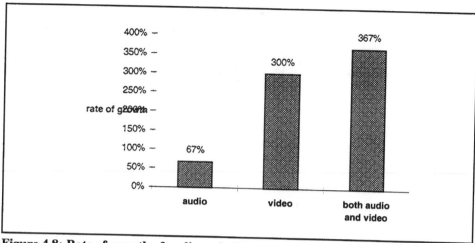

400% —
350% —
300% —
250% —
rate of g200%h —
150% —
100% —
50% —
0%

67%

300%

367%

audio

video

both audio
and video

Figure 4.8: Rate of growth of audio and video applications during the academic year 1996-1997

Hypothesis 5: Audio tools are:
a) more deployed than video, and
b) they are expanding faster

Survey Results

As depicted in the bar chart below, only 1 % of the respondents are using video while 8% are using audio. The rate of growth for audio tools is also higher than that for video tools (5% for audio versus 3% for video). These findings confirm hypothesis 5.

Question 8: Plans/Current Uses of The Internet for Course Delivery?

Background

As depicted earlier in Figure 4.5 and Figure 4.6, it is mainly the low cost, flexible tools which are predominating in a telelearning environment. These tools mainly include e-mail and its applications, the Web and text based conferencing tools.

With regards to e-mail, the most prevalent tool, it can be presumed that it is principally applied for asynchronous student/instructor and student/ student interactions. This type of interaction comprises: prolonged class discussions, virtual office hours, personal feedback, handing in assignments and quizzes, and students groupwork and projects.

Uses of the Web, which is almost as popular as e-mail, are mainly based on deploying the Web's hyperlinked environment. Many instructors, for instance, use the web as a repository for class material with hyperlinks to relevant information available on the Web. However, copyright issues prevent the posting of text books and other manuals on-line.

For students, the Web's vast information resources and its ubiquity provide them with a valuable tool for making searches and obtaining up to date up-to-the-minute information. Administrations of virtual institutions are also using the Web to provide information about the institution and the services it offers. Announcements and news are also posted on a web site for students and campus visitors.

Based on these facts the following hypotheses can be formulated:

Hypothesis 6: By comparison with all the other applications of the Internet within the telelearning environment, real time class lectures are the fastest growing functions.

Hypothesis 7: Hypertext manuals:
a) are not as widely used as lecture notes postings, and
b) their growth rate is lower than most of the other applications.

Survey Results

During the academic year 1995-1996, the Internet was mostly used for asynchronous communication, on-line class discussions and students feedback. In fact, respectively 69%, 62% and 59% of the respondents used the Internet for remote interaction, class discussions and feedback. Because of the high level of use of these applications, their growth rates for the academic year 1996-1997 are low since they have little opportunity to grow. Student communications has the lowest rate, (26%), followed by class discussions, (27%), and finally, student feedback, which has a rate of 31% increase.

Remote submissions of assignments and on-line lecture notes postings are also two widely applied functions of the Internet for on-line course delivery. Respectively, 54% of respondents use the net for handing in assignments electronically, and thereabouts the same proportion (53%) have web sites with the course on-line.

Although asynchronous interaction is very common between students and their instructor either on a group basis (on-line class discussions) or on an individual basis (virtual office hours and feedback), Internet tools are not as widely used for student-student interchanges, while working on cooperative assignments. Compared to 69% of the respondents who use the net for student-instructor communication, only 45% were using it for groupwork.

Concerning hypertext manuals, 37% of the respondents used the Internet to reproduce and post student manuals on-line. This rate is much lower however than simpler lecture notes postings, which are restricted in most of the cases to point format notes and cross references to other material. This result confirms the first part of hypothesis 7.

Remarkably, the growth of both applications is the same, 52%, and is one of the highest rates (the third highest). This outcome contradicts the second part of hypothesis 7. This can imply that despite the copyright issues, instructors are benefiting from powerful, simple-to-use filters and hypertext editors, which save them significant traditional delivery and time costs.

As expected the least employment of Internet tools is for on-line exams (19%), followed by real time lectures (15%). On the other side, both functions have the highest growth rate during 1996-1997: 69% for on-line exams and 59% for real time class lectures. These outcomes compare favorably with hypothesis 6.

These results are also in accordance with the answers of question 6, where real time conferencing tools, principally MUDs and MOOs, are the quickest expanding tools. Further, the reasons provided in the previous section about the possible reasons for the increased use of on-line lectures, strongly justify the 69% growth rate.

The option "other," where respondents were expected to provide supplementary uses of the Internet tool for a flexible on-line telelearning environment, is not included in the graph. Respondents identified the following functions:

- Used for interactive computer assisted instruction modules completed by the student, that replace class lectures.
- Used to download multimedia files, assignments and practice exams.
- Used it in a forum discussion format for group brainstorming, developed like a newsgroup.
- Case Study presentations by students using multimedia files.
- Using the on-line material as an adjunct to the traditional paper-based course guide, reinforcing it where appropriate and providing relevant material on-line for student use during labs.

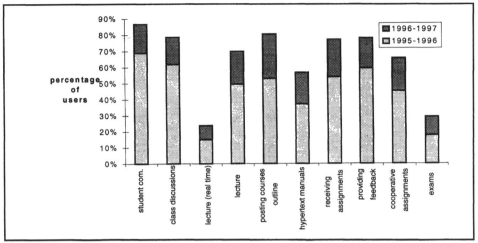

Figure 4.9: Percentage of users applying the suggested functions

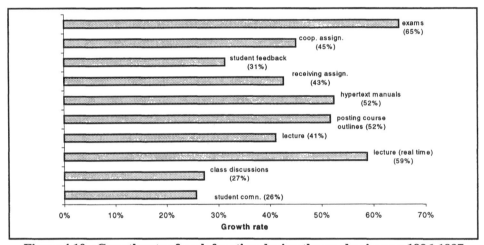

Figure 4.10 : Growth rate of each function during the academic year 1996-1997

Question 9: Advantages of Using the Internet for Teaching/Learning?

Background

The last two questions required users to give short answers about their opinions with regards to using the Internet within a telelearning environment, either as a complementary and integral tool or as the only fundamental system for on-line knowledge transfer.

Internet based learning offers a wealth of benefits to the teaching and telelearning community. The following are some of its main valuable services:

- It improves access to a wide, universal community of students: The Internet service today is more popular today than two years ago. Also the number of commercial service providers has grown, giving rise to competition, bringing down service costs, and resulting in opportunities for more people to access the technology. Moreover, because the Internet is based on standard communication protocols, and because much of its software can be downloaded directly, students and instructors around the world can be sure of compatibility regardless of the platforms they are using.
- It is a cost and time effective solution for delivering education and for accessing learning material. First, costs of the required equipment for telelearning via the Internet are, in most of the cases, a one-time investment and are continuously dropping in price. Also, many of the applications used can be downloaded for free directly from the Internet. Moreover, telelearning via the Internet saves the travel time and costs to go to class, as well as the extra buildings, and faculty costs. Compared with other distance learning methods, telelearning practitioners save the costs of courier services and traditional video-conferencing equipment.
- The relatively low cost electronic publishing and Internet access, combined with on-line flexible support services, such as those offered by the Global Network Academy, enable individual teachers wishing to teach without instructional support, to compete for students by giving stand alone on-line courses.
- Extended class discussions beyond lecture time, and the ability to review previous sessions provide students with more time for reflection, analyzing and writing neat responses. It also encourages active involvement of the whole group in the discussion. Further, it stimulates increased student-instructor interaction, which provides more support and help for students.
- As students are learning advanced tools and technologies, they are using most of the tools and developing the skills that will be an essential part of their work later.
- It is highly convenient: Teaching and learning via the Internet is highly flexible. Neither instructors nor students are confined by time or space, as they can access the Internet anytime from anywhere. Further, it permits students with special needs such as physically disabled people, or those with certain life and work conditions, to benefit from educational programs and to upgrade their skills.
- It is easy to use. Internet software smoothly integrates different resources, providing users with a simple and user-friendly interface, which is quickly and easily mastered.

- It improves learning resources. The Internet allows access to a readily available world-wide information resource, ideal for education and research. The ability of creating links to relevant resources, such as simulation software and multimedia documents, considerably supports teachers in their preparation of the course material and provides students with high quality learning resources.
- The ability to incorporate hypermedia, simulation software and real time multimedia applications provides considerable support for a telelearning environments. It permits the delivery of sophisticated instructional material to students anywhere. At the same time, using such tools improves the technological capabilities of students and instructors and helps them to get acquainted with the different features of the continuously developing Internet technologies.
- Internet material development is relatively easy, quick and low cost: development of instructional material and uploading it to the Net is easy and can be done very quickly. The HTML language used to do so is very easy to learn and provides several capabilities and options for presenting information in different formats. Further, unlike printed resources, the Internet presents a powerful tool for publishing and updating Internet information at low time and money costs.

Survey Results

The following is a list of the benefits the survey respondents believe the Internet provides for a telelearning on-line environment.

- It provides global access a large audience.
- It is flexible.
- It permits the easy processing of a large number of student tasks and provides self paced learning.
- It allows for more open discussions with people form all over the world;
- It allows *any one* to access and learn *any time* they wish to learn about nearly any subject.
- It allows for a global and fairly inexpensive education.
- It is time efficient in terms of reaching students and instructors any time and anywhere.
- It grants an easier, faster and more convenient communication between students, instructors and administration.
- It allows for a more efficient use of class time.

- It helps students develop new skills, such as: discussion, writing, thinking, collaboration, computer literacy, etc.
- It is of great value for isolated students/countries.
- It facilitates one-on-one tutoring, therefore allowing and encouraging students who might be reluctant to participate in class, but have equally valid points to make.
- It increases student motivation and involvement in the learning process;
- It provides a wealth of information resources for students and instructors;
- It has spurred creativity! It also allows for the most up-to-date information for research papers.
- Allows for a rapid generation of custom course materials in place of a standard textbook authored by the instructor.
- It provides up-to-date material and allows for frequent adjustments to course syllabus.
- It opens up a world of diversity and multi-culturism.

Question 10: Disadvantages of Using the Internet for Teaching/Learning?

Background

Despite the long list of the Internet benefits for on-line telelearning via the Internet, this medium also has some disadvantages and issues, which should be taken into consideration before implementing an on-line class via the Internet. Some of the main issues such as economics, security, accreditation and copyright will be discussed later in part IV. The following are some other minor issues, which can affect the efficiency of the telelearning environment to a certain extent. These include:

- Time difference between the different world areas can cause certain communication problems when using real time applications, limiting the effectiveness of these tools for some multinational groups.
- Increased developments of high bandwidth technologies require higher speed Internet access, which is not yet available at affordable prices in many areas around the world. This can deprive many students from using the Internet's powerful features and can limit access to some courses, e.g. where multimedia is very necessary such as medical classes.
- The vast information resources can deter students during their search for information and can easily result in information overload.

- The added responsibilities for on-line teachers may discourage many from pursuing this method of instruction, especially in the case of large classes.
- Many faculty members are concerned that the Internet can represent a threat to human resources, since one professor can serve thousands of students. This would reduce the number of faculty members and could result in a loss of diversity.
- Based on many Internet and computer users' experience, reading long documents over the computer monitor is not as comfortable as when reading a printed document at the reader's convenience. This can be explained by the fact that on-line documents have less resolution than paper. As a result, users incur extra printing costs which increases expenses of using the Internet medium for telelearning.
- Using the computer for too long can cause several health problems. Sitting for too long can result in back problems. Prolonged on-line reading sessions can stress the eyes. Using high keyboards, ill-fitting chairs, working in stressful conditions, typing for extended hours of typing, and frequent use of the mouse, can tear the muscles, nerves and tendons, which become irritated and inflamed. This problem is known as the Repetitive Strain Injury or RSI. All these health problems represent extra hidden costs for telelearning via the Internet.

Survey Results

Respondents had several comments about the shortcomings and problem areas of the medium, which need attention in arder to provide a problem free on-line environment. The main remark is that many of the issues that respondents were experiencing, such as security matters and technical problems like bandwidth and technical support, have been either solved or are being addressed.

The following are the main criticisms of the survey respondents:

- Much of the information available on the WWW is irrelevant, therefore students can easily have an information overload and can lead to a loss of time searching.
- Many technical problems including: connection, access to material, delays and cut off, slow downloading of multimedia files, low bandwidth.
- Time consuming technical problems.
- Lack of students and instructors computer literacy.
- Continuous need for technical support.

- Technical problems quickly lead to student frustration therefore affecting their concentration during the class session.
- Time zone problems.
- Searching can be cumbersome and clumsy.
- Some sites are not easy to access or disappear and change address.
- Lack of security.
- Increased workload for instructors.
- Current Internet tools are not fully adequate to students needs.
- Social campus aspects cannot be replicated.
- Paying for access is a problem for students.
- It is hard for instructors to keep discussions in harmony.
- High risk of flaming and inappropriate behavior during discussions.
- Academic resistance to this new way of teaching.

Conclusion

Based on the survey's outcomes, the main conclusions can be summarized as follows:

- The Internet's ubiquity and easy access, coupled with the increased developments and proliferation of its tools are opening up new opportunities for telelearning students and institutions, who have already started deploying the medium as a flexible learning environment.
- This concept is confirmed by the fact that by the academic year 1996-1997 almost all the respondents will be using the Internet as an integral tool of their course delivery. The institutions which were deploying the Internet for their educational delivery were not limited to only high level institutions such as universities and professional organizations but also involved colleges, primary and high schools.
- The main powerful aspect of the Internet which strongly encouraged our respondents to adopt the different Internet tools, is the easy reach to class members any time and anywhere, which resulted in improved communication between them. Furthermore, cost efficiency was also among the main reasons which invited users to use the Internet, in addition to the previously mentioned ones.
- Unlike what many people would think, our respondents did not consider that quick and easy research are among the most important reasons for implementing the Internet tools to support on-line course delivery.

- Given the current network limitations, and the high cost of broadband access, low bandwidth modules which mainly involved e-mail applications were the most prevalent tools used for on-line distribution of learning material. Real time text based tools, which provide flexible cyber environments and live interactions, principally MUDs and MOOs, on the other hand, are quickly increasing in popularity among the educational community. The real time video-conferencing software, such as CUSeeMe, is also being highly promoted, especially with the continuous upgrades in its technology. User education about the best ways of deploying these tools would grant users higher quality environments and an increased efficiency. Not until high speed connections become affordable and network issues are solved, would the majority of the telelearning community start adopting high bandwidth technologies such as the MBONE.
- Taking into account the network issues stated earlier and the scarcity of bandwidth, multimedia applications are limited to downloads of multimedia web files, to supplement presentations and research projects. The lack of standards is a significant discouraging factor for the widespread telelearning community to adopt these tools for on-line delivery of educational material. Analogous to the case of real time multimedia applications, network improvements would considerably promote the integration of these media.
- Despite the fact that many of the respondents still consider the Internet as being insecure, upgrades in the network security field, have been motivating other telelearning practitioners to use the medium for giving or taking on-line exams. Furthermore, the unsolved electronic material copyright issues did not really hinder many of our respondents from providing their students with on-line hypertext manuals.
- Despite the various advantages of using the Internet within a telelearning environment, several issues such as network security, bandwidth insufficiency and costly high speed connections are still presenting obstacles for a higher quality on-line educational environment and more efficient and smooth interactions. Hardware and software developers are currently working on solving these issues and on upgrading the medium and making it more convenient for the Internet user community including telelearning practitioners.

Other issues such as the ability to monitor on-line discussions, on-line class material preparation time and effort investments, training needs and technical support required are temporary issues which are solved soon as the users get more familiar with the tool and become able to use it smoothly.

Chapter 5

■

Yahoo! Internet Life
Survey Analysis

During the month of March 1997, Yahoo! Internet Life magazine, conducted a survey that ranked the most wired higher education institutions in the United States. The survey queried 300 colleges and universities on 35 different Internet related factors, organized under four main categories: hardware, academics, student affairs and social services. Answers to questions of the top 100 most wired institutions were published on-line, as well as an explanation of the method used for rating. While academics accounted for 45% of the total score, hardware and social use of the net each constituted 22.5%. Student services comprised 10%. Items such as the college web page content, aesthetics, or navigability were not taken into consideration, as it was believed that these can be very misleading in assessing the extent of available Net services to students.

The analysis of the findings was very brief, and there were no comments explaining the facts but a listing of percentages of the different answers. The accompanying article "America's 100 Most Wired Colleges," by Dina Gan, mainly talked about future expectations of the new wired educational environment, but there was no study of the present Net deployments. For that reason, we have studied the results by summarizing the survey's result of a selected set of the surveyed institutions, in a table. Next, we analyzed these results and deduced a set of conclusions about the new trend of on-line telelearning via the Internet. The data we selected includes the three top most wired educational institutions as well as some of the major universities at lower ranks, such as Stanford and Harvard universities. Our comments will only focus on the top 100 schools since no information was published about the other 200 schools. Results are classified according to the four categories in summary tables, followed by a discussion of the findings. We note that the majority of the questions were included, except a few which were not of immediate relevance to our subject.

Hardware and Wiring

Questions under this category intended to investigate elements such as: the proportion of student-owned computers vs. those which belong to school, the number of computers per student, Internet and on-line library access, e-mail accounts and server space for students' web pages.

Table 5.1 gives a snapshot of the Internet services offered by our selected set of institutions. The factors considered are:

• Student owned computers: this factor provides a percentage of the students who own the campus computers.
• Port to student ratio: this ratio is the number of ports available per student; best is 1:1.
• Default e-mail account: means that students automatically get an e-mail account.
• Web page: asks if students are automatically offered room for their own Web pages.
• Unlimited Web access: surveys whether students are offered unlimited Internet access or not. Since some schools require extra fees for use beyond a certain number of hours.
• On-line library access: investigates if students are having access to the campus library or not.

In many of the surveyed institutions, students can own the campus computers, while others belong to the school. Percentages vary widely as we go down the ranking, raging between 100% down to only 10%. Despite that, we notice that the port to student ratio was very good (1:1) in most of the listed schools in our table and in 75% of the whole group. These results reflect that the majority of these schools have the adequate level of computer resources to support an on-line networked environment. Schools with low ratios, explained that funding problems are the main constraints of achieving the 1:1 ratio.

When it comes to on-line access to library catalogs, unlimited Web

Rank	College name	Student owned computers (%)	Port to student ratio	Default e-mail account	Web page	Unlimited web access	On-line library access
1	MIT	80	1:1	YES	YES	YES	YES
2	North Western	90	1:1	YES	YES	YES	YES
3	Emerson	90	1:1	YES	YES	YES	YES
5	Dartmouth	100	1:1	YES	YES	YES	YES
6	U. of Oregon	50	1:1	YES	YES	YES	YES
7	NJIT	100	1:1	YES	YES	YES	YES
17	U of Berkeley	75	3:4	YES	NO	YES	YES
50	Cornell U.	80	1:1	YES	YES	YES	YES
55	U of Michigan	60	2:3	YES	YES	YES	YES
57	NYU	60	1:3	YES	YES	YES	YES
60	YALE	80	1:1	YES	YES	YES	YES
64	HARVARD	97	1:1	YES	YES	YES	YES
78	UCLA	55	1:1	YES	NO	YES	YES
84	Stanford	40	1:1	YES	YES	YES	YES
100	Milsaps	10	1:1	YES	YES	YES	YES

Table 5.1 : Summary of responses to the Hardware and Wiring category (derived from Yahoo Internet Life, March 1997)

access, default e-mail and student Web pages, we notice that these applications have become a guaranteed service for students, and that institutions are encouraging wide Internet access. Figures recorded that all the institutions offer on-line library access, 99% offer unlimited web access, 98% offer default e-mail accounts and 87% offer students Web space for home pages.

Academics

This is the most important and weighty category, which judged how well an institution is using the Internet for on-line teaching and learning. The factors considered are the on-line use of classes of the Internet for Web pages, on-line homework and on-line study aids.

The first observation is that, as we go down in the ranking, the use of the Net for on-line class activities decreases and is not available in several cases. For instance, while all the courses at Dartmouth University and 80% of classes at the University of Oregon have Web pages, only 5% and 6% of the classes, respectively at Stanford University and at UCLA offer on-line services. No class at Harvard University, has an on-line element. These results can be explained by several facts. First, as admitted by many administrators at institutions with low ratios, much of their faculties "are still averse to this stuff (i.e. the Internet)". Several institutions can view the Internet as a threat to their autonomy and a means of diluting and homogenizing standards. For individual universities, such as Stanford and Harvard Universities,

Rank	College name	Classes with web pages (%)	Classes with on-line homework (%)	Classes with on-line study aids (%)
1	MIT	40	90	60
2	North Western	60	40	60
3	Emerson	50	55	60
5	Dartmouth College	100	100	100
6	U. of Oregon	80	40	40
7	NJIT	33	12.5	25
17	U of Berkeley	40	N/A	40
50	Cornell U.	N/A	N/A	N/A
55	U. of Michigan	25	N/A	N/A
57	NYU	5	2	2
60	YALE	10	7.5	N/A
64	HARVARD	N/A	N/A	N/A
78	UCLA	6	N/A	N/A
84	Stanford	5	2	5
100	Milsaps College	5	5	20

Table 5.2 Summary of responses to the Academics category (derived from Yahoo Internet Life, March 1997)

putting their course on-line for the open public would mean the loss of their distinctive flavor and an over-standardization of courses.

Smaller and less popular universities can use the Internet as a powerful marketing medium, which helps accessing the large universal "market of students," and therefore increasing their enrollment rate. Bigger institutions on the other hand, which want to preserve their face-to-face tradition, would simply use their reputation as a factor to attract more students.

Colleges and universities which are already offering distance education and lifelong learning programs and courses, such Dartmouth College, have very high academic scores. These institutions are using the medium to offer their remote students a flexible learning setting, where they can access their class lectures any time and anywhere and they can fulfill their class requirements on-line. Other institutions with low academic scores, are willing to go on-line and are already in the process of doing so.

Student Services

Questions under this category, looked into the use of the Internet for student affairs. These included on-line registration, on-line add and drop of courses, on-line transcripts and on-line syllabi. The following table summarizes the responses of the selected group of institutions.

Of the 100 most wired American colleges and universities, only 29% allow for on-line registration and 28% allow on-line add and drop of courses.

Rank	College name	On-line registration	On-line add/drop	On-line transcript	On-line syllabi
1	MIT	YES	YES	NO	YES
2	North Western	NO	NO	YES	YES
3	Emerson	YES	YES	YES	YES
5	Dartmouth	YES	YES	NO	YES
6	U. of Oregon	YES	YES	YES	YES
7	NJIT	YES	YES	YES	YES
17	U. of Berkeley	YES	YES	YES	YES
50	Cornell U.	YES	YES	YES	YES
55	U. of Michigan	YES	YES	YES	YES
57	NYU	NO	NO	YES	YES
60	YALE	NO	NO	NO	YES
64	HARVARD	NO	NO	YES	YES
78	UCLA	NO	NO	YES	YES
84	Stanford	YES	YES	YES	YES
100	Milsaps	NO	NO	YES	YES

Table 5.3 Summary of responses to the Student services category questions (derived from Yahoo Internet Life, March 1997)

On the other hand, 43% of these institutions allow students to view their transcripts on-line and 100% have on-line syllabi and summary of their offered programs. Many respondents stated that security and privacy are the two main factors which limited the use of the Internet for certain student services such as accessing grades and transcripts. Usually, this type of information is considered very sensitive and personal for students, but the Internet environment is still not percieved to be sufficiently secure to guarantee private transmission of this information to students. Syllabi, on the other hand, which provide web site visitors with general information about the institution are available at all institutions since they do not present any security concerns for administrators. Such results, along with the Internet security and privacy reasons, can explain why the weight of this category is the lowest, since providing private information on-line is not an adequate factor to judge an institution's on-line services. A case in point is Dartmouth college, which scores very high in academics but it still does not allow on line transmission of transcripts.

Social Services

The last series of questions examined the different on-line social services offered for students. Some of these factors we considered in our summary are the possibility of having student web pages on the school's Web system, club Web pages, on-line chatting, events listings and newsgroups. Table 5.4 summarizes the results of our selected set of institutions.

Rank	College name	Student web pages	Club web pages (%)	On-line gaming/chat	Events listing	Newsgroup hierarchy
1	MIT	YES	100%	YES	YES	YES
2	North Western	YES	70	YES	YES	YES
3	Emerson	YES	80	YES	YES	YES
5	Dartmouth	YES	70	YES	YES	YES
6	U. of Oregon	YES	80	YES	NO	YES
7	NJIT	YES	100	YES	YES	YES
17	UC Berkeley	NO	90	NO	YES	NO
50	Cornell U.	NO	90	NO	YES	NO
55	U of Michigan	YES	80	NO	YES	YES
57	NYU	YES	60	NO	NO	YES
60	YALE	NO	33	YES	YES	YES
64	HARVARD	YES	80	NO	YES	YES
78	UCLA	NO	50	YES	YES	YES
84	Stanford U.	YES	25	YES	NO	YES
100	Milsaps	YES	20	NO	YES	YES

Table 5.4: Summary of results for the Social Services category questions (derived from Yahoo Internet Life, March 1997)

As portrayed above in table 5.4, and based on results for the whole group of the 100 most wired institutions, most social services are available in almost all the institutions, except for the on-line gaming and chat. Results report that 85% of the most wired institutions host a campus-based newsgroup hierarchy and 87% offer students Web space for a home page. When comparing results in other categories, we notice that institutions with high academic scores also have the highest scores and the maximum number of on-line social services. This can be explained by the fact that many students will be spending much of their time on the Net. Therefore browsing the institutional site, posting other institution related information such as events advertisements and club announcements, allows the remote student to be informed about the institution's activities like any other students on campus. Moreover, newsgroup hierarchies and chatting sessions complete the scene of a virtual campus environment.

Many of the surveyed institutions however, discourage extracurricular services, especially on-line gaming and chatting, as they are a "drag on resources", as one administrator puts it. Another staff member stated that the reason why his institution is not keen on on-line chatting is that they "don't want to facilitate chat groups that pertain to all manner of things that have nothing to do with education."

Conclusion

Based on this survey's results, we came to the conclusion that a growing number of American institutions are integrating the Internet within their learning environment. At this time, unlimited access to the Internet, the WWW and on-line libraries, as well as a default e-mail account and campus based newsgroups are becoming guaranteed services for American students. However, several institutions are still very wary when it comes to administrative services, such as on-line registration, on-line transcripts and course selection.

Despite the increased use of the Internet among major academic institutions, certain universities especially distinctive ones, such as Harvard and Stanford universities, are not keen on using this medium for on-line education. Face to face settings can therefore be expected to be used for the foreseeable future, and there will always be people and institutions that favor the traditional setting over the emerging virtual telelearning environment.

Conclusion to Part II

The academic environment is undergoing trends, which are reshaping it and are resulting in the emergence of new forms of instruction and learning and new academic structures. These trends can be classified into teaching and learning trends and organizational trends.

Teaching and Learning Trends

The first main teaching and learning trend, as portrayed in the two surveys and case studies, is the fact that many of the Internet tools are becoming an integral part of the education process, primarily e-mail and its different applications and the Web. At the same time, a rapid evolution is taking place from low bandwidth asynchronous applications such as e-mail and text-based, real-time conferencing tools such as IRC, and MUDs and MOOs, towards higher bandwidth multimedia on demand and real time applications such as multimedia e-mail, multimedia 3D MUDs and MOOs, and conferencing tools such as CUSeeMe. Despite this progress, issues like security, copyright and the open access to low quality Internet material, still limit the use of the Internet for sensitive operations such as accessing educational material, on-line fee payments, on-line registration, and on-line transcripts.

The second significant trend is the increased use of multicast capabilities. Current applications primarily use multimedia-conferencing tools such as CUSeeMe. The new MBONE technology on the other hand, is still not familiar to the surveyed institutions. This can be explained by the experimental stage of the technology and the lack of support to the new multicasting protocol by the ISPs.

Organizational Trends

When it comes to the organizational trends, the surveys revealed that many educational institutions are increasingly offering on-line services, programs and degrees to the worldwide learning community. This new direction in their strategy will play a significant role in increasing the enrollment rate of students and might even help them solve some of their financial problems.

At the same time, a new form of academic institution has emerged, which is totally on-line and uses the Internet for all faculty operations and teaching activities, including lectures, testing, discussions, etc. Furthermore, the rise of on-line, flexible support services, such as those offered by the Global Network Academy, combined with the relatively low cost electronic publishing and Internet access, has encouraged many individual teachers wishing to teach without instructional support, to offer stand alone on-line courses.

Finally, one important remark about the deployment of the Internet is that almost all the respondents and the available case studies were from the USA followed by Canada, and then Europe. This assertion is confirmed by the last survey of the Graphic, Visualization, & Usability Center's (GVU) 6th WWW User Survey, which reported that 83% of Web users are from the US, 6% come from Europe, and just under 6% from Canada and Mexico. This fact can be explained by the wide and easy access to the medium in these areas of the world compared with other countries.

Part III

■

Economics of Telelearning
Via the Internet

Costing the use of the Internet technology for telelearning is a difficult and complex task for two major reasons. First, the international aspect of the Internet technology, and the worldwide access to on-line resources adds significant complications to the costing procedure, as it is very difficult to develop universal costing measures. Second, with the rapid technological developments of the Internet tools and applications, cost structures are continuously evolving.

Limitless options and scenarios of applying Internet tools are available, which adds complexity to the costing process. For instance, costing a course using a combination of text, multimedia and live audio/video which is being multicast to participants who are also using different combinations of tools and access methods, can be very intricate. The fact also that telelearners are, very probably, scattered all over the world, adds extra complications, since prices and charges of cost elements such as equipment, access charges, wages and many other related costs, vary widely from one country to another.

Likewise, the increased competition among the different telecommunication companies has lead to a wide variety of charges and access options. Furthermore, there is very little information about how current costs and charges such as tuition fees, instructors and tutors fees, etc. are set by virtual institutions.

In view of all these facts, attempting today to provide a general purpose cost analysis of telelearning via the Internet can easily result in conclusions which do not reflect correctly the actual incurred expenses.

Because of these difficulties, this chapter does not attempt to present hard dollar figures. Instead it identifies some common elements in the cost structure of an Internet-based telelearning system. These elements are categorized under institution related costs and student related costs. The dollar figures given are current only at the time of writing, and should be used to compare among options, not as a means of performing an accurate cost analysis.

The student related costs include:

• Internet access costs.
• Tuition fees.
• Other costs such as print material and courier costs.

The institution related costs comprise mainly:

• Planning and preparing the institution's strategy and general policies.
• Equipment costs, which includes hardware and software.
• Site construction costs.
• Technical support costs.
• Instructors and tutors costs, which involve: training, compensation and possible extra remuneration costs for upgrading and developing the on-line programs.
• Maintenance and upgrades costs of computer servers, as new technologies are developed.

Generally, the total costs incurred when setting up a telelearning environment via the Internet, depend on the strategy implemented by the educational institution, and on the Internet access technology chosen by on-line students. For instance, costs of an institution offering a few courses on-line would be different from an entirely on-line institution. Also, expenses of delivering educational material to a hybrid group of on-line and on campus students are higher than the case where all the students are interacting remotely. Further, a student accessing the Internet using a 28.8 Kbps modem will have less expensive, but a slower connection than another, who is using an ISDN line connection.

In our discussion, institution related costs such as computer labs, accommodations, regular staff salaries, etc. will not be included. Instead, only costs directly related to instituting a telelearning environment via the Internet will be considered.

Configuration of an On-line Academic Institution

Figure 6.1 illustrates a sample connection of a virtual educational on-line institution, where remote students, who can be scattered in different areas around the world, connect to the Web server and access the institution's resources through the Internet. The Web server is linked to the institution's LAN, which is connected to the Internet, through its ISP.

The following chapters will provide a more detailed explanation about the different cost elements related to students (Chapter 6) and institutions (Chapter 7). [Note: All costs are in terms of US dollars.]

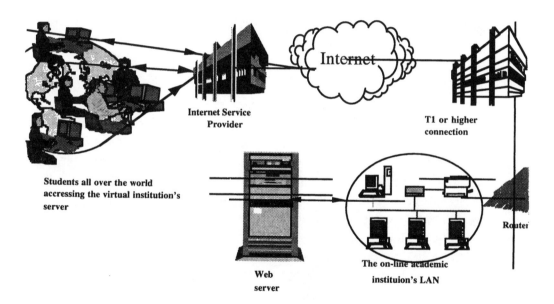

Figure 6.1: Sample configuration of a virtual institution

Chapter 6

■

Student Related Costs

Costs incurred by students include the following three elements:

Internet access: This section includes a description of the different options available today, for accessing the Internet. Although most of these technologies, such as ADSL and cable modem, are still at an early stage, the promising opportunities they offer for high speed connections to students with limited budgets, implies that it is very likely that on-line students will be using them. Fast technological developments, competition among telecommunication companies, and the urgent need for affordable high speed connections, imply that these technologies will very soon be available for telelearners. [*Remark:* When costs are calculated for each technology, the cost of the computer terminal and the TCP/IP software will not be considered, since they are a common basic requirement for all access options. Both costs are one-time expenses. They are estimated to have the following values.]

Tuition fees: which vary widely today between one on-line institution to another.

Other costs: such as courier costs of hard copy learning materials, and encryption keys expenses, as well as other costs which are charged to students by some on-line institutions.

Internet Access

Having an Internet access is obviously a fundamental requirement for students willing to take a course or a degree via the Internet. The technology used to connect depends on several circumstances, such as program and

COST ELEMENT	TOTAL COSTS US$	NOTES
Computer (Mac or PC)	1500	• Minimum Pentium processor, and at least 16 MBytes of memory.
TCP/IP software	50	• Needed to communicate on the Internet. • Sometimes provided by the Internet service provider.
Total initial Internet connection costs	1550	• Costs can be lower with the decline of computer prices.

Table 6.1 : Common cost elements of an Internet connection

students needs, availability of the technology and the on-line students' budgets. For instance, some on-line lectures might just require an e-mail account and the ability to carry on a text based real time interaction, in which case a connection using a 28.8 Kbps modem can be adequate. In other cases, upgrades in connection might be required as multimedia tools and broad bandwidth applications are becoming more common and essential in a telelearning environment.

The first option for students to have an Internet access, is to have it through the academic institution (this is in case the institution offers both conventional and on-line classes). Many academic institutions offering telelearning courses, provide their on-line students with an e-mail account, which can be accessed only through the institution's network. The institution makes an arrangement with a local ISP to provide students with dial-up accounts. On-line students registered at the institution, get extra hours and depending on the ISP package, they can be offered free access. The ISP provides all the modem access and troubleshooting. By having this type of access, the student only bears the expenses of the necessary equipment and tools for making the connections; these include: a personal computer, a modem with communication software and a phone line.

The second option to have Internet access, is when telelearners make the necessary arrangements on their own with an ISP, in which case they bear the extra costs of accessing the Internet. This option provides the student with a more flexible use of the Internet. Moreover, the expanding popularity of the Internet is pulling ISP charges down, while providing Internet users with more attractive access packages. Generally, virtual institutions expect that students make their own arrangements for their Internet connection.

The following sections describe the different Internet access technologies, which are either already available for use or are at an early stage of deployment. Choosing the most convenient technology depends on several considerations such as: access and installation charges and the availability of the technology to the telelearner.

Dial in modems

The most popular and most affordable way for student to get an Internet access is using analog phone lines and a modem. Dial-up connections are the easiest and most affordable way to connect a computer to the Internet. Given the increased use of multimedia Internet files and broad bandwidth applications, such as real time audio and video-conferencing, and new technologies such as Java, VRML, Shockwave, the need for higher speed connections is becoming a very basic requirement.

The first option for the student in order to get a faster Internet access is to upgrade his/her modem to a higher speed. The 28.8 Kbps modems have been widely used during the last year, and are selling at affordable prices less than $100. The more recent higher speed modems, which are rapidly expanding in use, at this time, are the 33.6 and 56 Kbps modems.

The 28.8, 33.6 and 56 Kbps modems transmission rates, coupled with the built in data compression of about 2:1 for ordinary text data and by up to 4:1 for some types of data, bring in more convenience for students with limited budgets. For instance, on-line time can dramatically decrease as transmission rate increases. The faster modems help students navigate the Web quicker, receive multimedia file attachments faster and get their homework done within a shorter time frame. As a result, telelearners can benefit better from the Web resources while saving on telephone and access charges.

A wide variety of 33.6 and 56 Kbps modems is available, today, selling for under $200. Most of them maintain compatibility with older modulation protocols, and are easy to set up and use. They also offer attractive combinations of features such as voice mail, and full duplex speaker-phones, which are very useful for on-line audio and video-conferences. The cost of upgrading to 33.6 and 56 Kbps for those who currently own lower speed modems is minimal. Many modem makers are offering upgrades for a nominal fee.

One point to note, though, is that fast modems still have some performance problems. An analog telephone line has an upper limit to the amount of information it can transport. Despite their 33.6, 56 Kbps nominal speed, these modems are limited by the quality of the analog connection and routinely go no faster than 26.4 or 28.8 Kbps. This implies that, in order to acquire higher speed access, technologies other than modems should be used.

In order for users to benefit from the new high-speed modems ISPs need also to make software and hardware changes to their remote access servers and may need to increase capacity on their network backbone.

The new technology, however, still has several drawbacks and several problem areas to be untangled. Unlike all previous modem standards, 56 Kbps modems lack full-duplex capability. The 56 Kbps rate can only be achieved downstream to the remote user, while the upstream limit is 33.6 Kbps. For telelearners, downloading or receiving multimedia from their peers is not a big concern. The issue is for two way communication, such as during on-line lectures and discussions, using video and data conferencing. It is important to note that a 56 Kbps modem does not give the same audio and video quality in both directions.

Several companies are currently working on these issues and new solutions are emerging. One of the latest technologies, for instance, permits for symmetrical mode, which transmits data at 45 Kbps in both: the down-stream and upstream directions. This improvement will allow for more applications requiring fast rate transmissions, such as real time live lectures and multimedia file exchanges.

Costs for Students

When a modem is used for Internet access, the only involved cost is that of purchasing the modem. No installation by a technician or maintenance fees are required. Price, does not always reflect the quality and the performance of a modem, however. An on-line student needs a good high-speed modem which is able to get the most out of the current modulation specification, handle noisy telephone lines, work with a wide variety of file types with fidelity, and utilize the latest features that the phone networks offer.

The increasing availability of the 56 Kbps modems, and their affordable prices, and multiple conveniences promise on-line telelearning students and instructors wide opportunities for operating more effective real time lectures.

First, the anticipated costs of these modems are $200 when they were first introduced, and are now dropping to under $100. This means that an on-line student can acquire a more powerful modem than the commonly used ones at nearly the same price. Moreover, unlike other high speed technologies such as ISDN (in case an ISDN and a regular telephone are required), 56 Kbps modems require no special complex configuration or special services from the telephone company. Consequently, users will not incur any line installation fees, and do not have to go through the configuration and installation processes. Their responsibility is limited to the minimal equipment upgrades.

Furthermore, in order to save users the costs of new investments as standards develop and technology changes, 56 Kbps modem developers have designed the new modem technology so that:

• They are backwards compatible with existing 28.8 Kbps and 33.6 Kbps modem technology, and
• That it is software upgradable. This means that modems can be upgraded by downloading software via the Internet.

With all these upgrades and developments in the high modem speed rates, which are on the way of overcoming many of the new technologies drawbacks, the 56 Kbps data rate seems likely to establish itself as the main modem standard. Major ISPs support it, providing Internet users, primarily the on-line educational community, with high speed access and better real time services.

The following sections describe three of the fast emerging high bandwidth technologies, which can represent potential possibilities either now or in the near future for the on-line educational community. These are ISDN, ADSL and Cable modems.

ISDN: Integrated Services Digital Network

Compared to other high-speed technologies which are likely to be considered when choosing an affordable Internet access, ISDN is the most mature and widely available technology. ISDN is a digital telephone service, which works over the existing telephone lines and can carry voice, data, fax and video.

There are two types of ISDN services. The most appropriate type for individual computer users is the ISDN Basic Rate Interface (BRI) illustrated in Figure 6.2. BRI divides the telephone line into 3 digital channels: two 64 Kbps B (or Bearer) channels, and one 16 Kbps D (or Data) signaling channel. The B channels can carry data or voice or both. Telephone companies, in general, provide ISDN users with the options available for regular telephone calls, such as call display, call forwarding, long distance discounts etc. B channels can be bonded to act as a single 128 Kbps channel, providing a connection up to four times faster than the standard modem connection. (Bonding is an acronym for Bandwidth On Demand Interoperabiltiy Group). The D channel handles the administrative work such as setting up and tearing

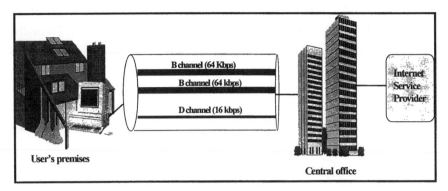

Figure 6.2: Elements of an ISDN connection and the different ISDN channels

down the call and communicating with the telephone network.

ISDN Advantages

ISDN popularity is attributed to several advantages:

- *High quality connections:* ISDN uses digital signals, which prevent the noise often affecting analog conversations and offers high quality communications worldwide.
- *High speed transmission and applications:* The commonly available modems have a maximum speed of 56 Kbps, but are limited to the quality of the analog connections and in many cases transmission cannot exceed 28.8 Kbps. ISDN, however, allows multiple digital channels to operate simultaneously through the standard phone wiring reaching a speed of 128 Kbps, when bonding is applied. This extra bandwidth is valuable for heavy Internet users, such as telelearners, especially when downloading and uploading multimedia files, browsing graphics and animated Web pages, and holding video-conferences.
- *Multiple services:* Before the introduction of ISDN, it was necessary to have a phone line for each device a user wants to use simultaneously, such as telephone, fax and computer. Technically, ISDN refers to the delivery of a specific set of digital services through a single interface. By applying ISDN, several data sources can be combined and routed to their proper destinations.
- *Signaling:* Instead of the ring voltage sent to ring the bell of the user's bell, ISDN sends a digital packet on the D channel. This signal does not disturb established connections, and call set up time is very fast. To illustrate, ISDN uses less than 2 seconds to establish a connection, while a modem takes 30-

60 seconds. The received signal indicates the caller, the dialed number and the type of the call (data/voice). This method of signaling is very useful for telelearners especially when performing multiple activities at the same time.

• *Acceptable rates:* Compared with dial-in modems limited convenience, ISDN monthly charges of about $50 to $80, are acceptable, especially when the telephone company acts as the ISP where ISDN and Internet access charges are combined into one fee. Likewise, ISDN hardware is constantly falling in prices and extra installation costs are applied occasionally, in case the user requires an extra telephone line

Issues with ISDN

Unlike analog telephone services, ISDN is not yet ubiquitous. While most urban and suburban areas have access to ISDN services, most rural areas are not served yet. Even in some urban areas, users may not be able to get the service. In order to have an ISDN connection, the local phone company has to install an ISDN interface plus some ISDN software on the switch in its central offices. Even if all the required equipment is installed at its central office, there are distance limitations on the access line, since ISDN works only within a radius of 18000 feet radius from the central office, or the telephone company's remote equipment (see Figure 6.3).

One other issue is that there should not be any problem with the wiring,

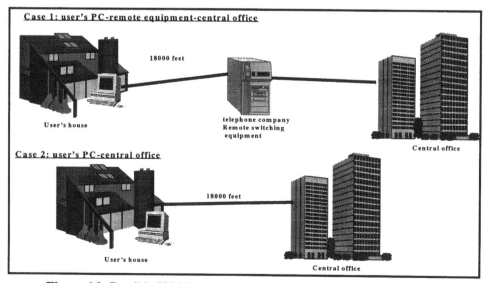

Figure 6.3: Possible ISDN connections between the user's premises and the telephone company's central office

which might interfere with the transmission. To prevent these problems, usually the phone company performs a "line qualification" to determine whether the user's wiring will support ISDN or not.

In order to overcome the distance and interference problems, some telephone companies are offering today, a service called "ISDN Anywhere". Under this service, even if the telephone company doesn't have the right equipment in the users' local central office, it tries to serve them from another exchange using "line extension" technology. This option allows more users to get the ISDN services, but at a significantly high cost. This implies that many telelearners can be deprived of the ISDN. Fortunately, many areas around the world are expanding their support to this technology, which promises an easier access to a larger number of users.

Another problem is that sometimes even if the phone company offers the ISDN services, not all ISPs offer ISDN access. Even those who provide ISDN, usually support a limited variety of ISDN equipment. This problem, however, is on its way to being solved, as ISDN service is becoming more common and demand for high speed access is increasing. Most ISPs, today, are more motivated to open up their networks for ISDN services, especially with the increased competition from telephone companies who are starting to operate as ISPs. The increased competition, is very likely to improve services for end users, and to bring access costs down. This would of great benefit for the Internet-based telelearning community with limited budgets.

One occasional problem, is that the process of installing an ISDN line is complex and time consuming. Unlike normal analog phone lines, an ISDN line provides many options and choices which must be defined in advance in order for the line to function. It is this increased flexibility which adds complexity to the ISDN line configuration. As the telephone companies are standardizing to a few preset configurations, and many ISDN equipment manufacturers are starting to support more provisioning configurations, this problem will be soon eliminated.

Finally, one point to watch for when using ISDN, is that an ISDN line connection through the ISP won't speed Internet access much, if the provider is over saturated; that is if the line is always busy or the user just can't get a response. This issue can be substantial in case of real time class discussions, where students are scattered in different areas around the globe.

Expanding international usage promises a big potential of the ISDN. Today most of Europe and Japan offers ISDN, although in North America the current focus is on ADSL, see below.

Requirements for an ISDN Service

In order to have access to ISDN services, the following steps are required:

• First, the user should check with the local phone company if ISDN service is available in the user's area. In many cases, the user would need to live near the phone company switching office for the line to have sufficient quality for digital transmissions.
• Then, they should verify if the ISP supports ISDN and if it offers an ISDN Internet dial up.
• In case a Plain Old Telephone Service (POTS) telephone is needed in addition to the ISDN telephone, the telephone company should install an additional line to the user's premises.

To fully utilize ISDN speed, a powerful personal computer with high speed serial port and convenient hardware and software are required. Windows 95 has various features supporting ISDN, including its special ISDN accelerator pack bonus.

• A terminal adapter or ISDN modem should be also installed. These devices, which come in external or internal models, include several interesting features. For instance, many models include an analog port, which allows the connection to fax machines and telephony devices. Hence, the user can utilize the ISDN line for both data and analog phone traffic. Other features comprise: voice and data calls, remote access to LANs, telecommuting, BBS access, groupware, and large file transfers. ISDN equipment prices are dropping rapidly. Terminal adapters can now be purchased for under $200.
• Finally, in addition to the ISDN service and hardware, software is required to enable the adapter to be integrated with other parts of the operating system. The most common way to provide connectivity over ISDN lines, is using the Point to Point Protocol (PPP), which is the protocol typically used to access the Internet. Windows 95, Windows NT or later versions, offer native support for PPP and ISDN. This results in an easy software configuration, higher performance, and an excellent interoperability with a broad range of ISDN equipment. Some ISDN service providers offer technical support for hardware and software installation for a fee.

Figure 6.4 illustrates the internal wiring in a user's house and the required ISDN equipment.

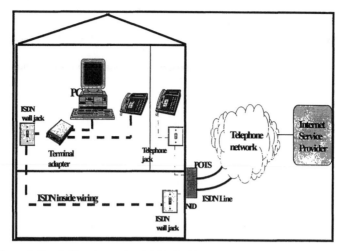

Source: http://www.bell.ca/bell/eng/promo/zap/wiringdoc.htm

Figure 6.4: Internal wiring for an ISDN connection with an ISDN and a POTS telephones

Costs for Students

An ISDN service charges consists of 4 components:

Access charges:
The access charges usually depend on the user's location and how the user was provided the service (i.e. whether the telephone company used a line extension or not). Access charges include two portions:

• *A monthly fixed charge*: recurring each month for having access to the ISDN line. This is of the order of $50 per month.
• *A usage charge* which varies depending on the amount of time spent using the line. Typically, it is not more than a couple of cents per minute for local calls with a maximum cap of about $50/channel/month. The monthly charge may include a certain number of hours of free usage each month. Some packages have no usage charges at all, or may waive usage charges during evenings and weekends.

Terminal requirements costs
These are one time start up costs, and they include:

• *Terminal costs:* Which is the cost of the terminal adapter. These are usually bought from the ISP or the telephone company. for about $300, depending

Cost Element	Total cost	Notes
Installation charges: Terminal requirements	$30 $300	ISDN jack installation for 1 hour inside wiring terminal adapter Software installation and configuration costs: $50
Total start up costs:	$330	
Access charges Internet service provider	$50 + $50 $20	Cost components involve: Monthly fixed charge + usage charge of $1.00/hr/channel with a cap of $50/channel Typical ISP rate.
Total monthly charges:	$120	

Table 6.2: Summary of costs of an ISDN connection

on the performance, quality and features.

- *Software installation and configuration costs*: As mentioned above, with Windows 95, the software installation and configuration can be done easily. However, the user might still need support and advice about the new service. Many telephone companies offer the help of a qualified service technician to do all the hardware and software installation and configuration.
- *Internet Service Provider:* Since many ISPs are offering the ISDN service as part of their package, they usually charge the same rates as to standard modem rates. The increased competition among ISPs and with telephone companies offering Internet services, is providing users with very attractive and low cost packages. The average ISP rates are about $20/month. Some ISPs monthly fees today are as low as $10.00 to about $30.0 depending on the amount of access time. Most ISPs today, offer the bonding option, where the rate is doubled to 128 Kbps. Such connections are usually tracked as double connection time, and therefore the cost is doubled.

Table 6.2 summarizes the different cost elements of the Internet access using an ISDN line.

Despite the high transmission rates offered by ISDN, live interactive video-conferencing sessions can be low quality especially when the session heavily uses extra multimedia material and applications. Full motion video requires upwards of 1.5 Mbps using MPEG compression (Motion Pictures Expert Group) which is far beyond basic rate ISDN data rates, and even transmission of large graphics files is slow.

Taking into account ISDN's limitations, combined with the elevated demand for high speed access and broad bandwidth applications, telephone companies have been working on a more powerful technology, which can

Data rate	Distance	Wire size
1.544 Mbps	up to 18,000 feet	0.5 mm
2.048 Mbps	16,000 feet	0.4 mm
6.312 Mbps	12,000 feet	0.5 mm
8.448 Mbps	9,000 feet	0.4 mm
	Source: http://198.93.24.23/ADDL_Tutorial.html	

Table 6.3: Downstream ADSL data rates depending on distance

guarantee high quality transmission of full motion video at affordable rates. This technology is ADSL.

ADSL: Asymmetric Digital Subscriber Line

ADSL is a recently developed modem technology, which uses the existing twisted pair telephone lines for multimedia and high speed data communication delivery. As its name implies, ADSL transmits an asymmetric data stream, with a high downstream rate from the network of up to 9 Mbps, and an upstream rate to the network up to 640 Kbps. Unlike an ISDN or a dial up modem, ADSL modems are constantly connected to the Net as long as the computer is on. Among other services such as video on demand, high speed Internet access is one of the principal services to be offered.

ADSL modems have been tested successfully by more than 30 telephone companies in North America and Europe and service is available in selected cities.

An ADSL circuit connects a pair of ADSL modems on each end of a twisted-pair telephone line, one at the telephone company's central office and the other at the customer premises, over a standard telephone line. This circuit provides three channels, as shown in Figure 6.5:

1. A high speed downstream channel: ranging from 1.5 up to 9 Mbps, and
2. A medium speed duplex channel: ranging form 16 Kbps to 640 Kbps.
   Each one of these channels can be sub-multiplexed to form multiple, lower rate channels.
3. and a POTS (Plain Old Telephone Service) channel, which carries the regular analog telephone conversations. The POTS channel is separated from the digital modem by filters, leaving POTS service independent and undisturbed, even if a premises ADSL modem fails.

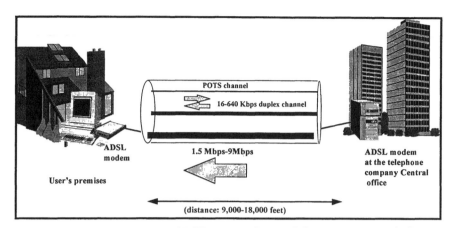

Figure 6.5: Structure of the ADSL connection and data rate transmissions

The downstream data rates depend on a number of factors, including the distance between the user and the telephone company central office, the copper wire guage and the presence of bridged taps.

Table 6.3 gives the different ranges of downstream data rates depending on distance.

Premises beyond these distances can be reached with fiber or copper Digital Loop Carrier Systems (DLCS). Telephone companies are convinced that they can offer ubiquitous ADSL access in a relatively short time.

Advantages of ADSL

There are several benefits of the ADSL technology based modems. The following are some of these advantages :

• *Service guarantee regardless of distance or loop:* This is a very important feature to keep smooth and continuous communication, especially during on-line live lectures. The ADSL modem will always connect. First, it attempts connection at the maximum rate (e.g., 9 Mbps). If the line condition does not permit connection at this bandwidth, it will then attempt to reestablish connection at successively lower data rates, until a solid connection is established. If no other connections are possible, it falls back to the lowest data rate, typically 1.5 Mbps. Thus, on-line lecture sessions are always assured continuous transmission. This represents a very advantageous and significant feature for on-line institutions, since high quality service would encourage more students to take on-line classes.

• *Automatic evaluation of line capacity, without any service provider inter-*

vention: This is very beneficial since it reduces maintenance expenses. For example, in case a line over-saturates, ADSL modems alert the user's system, thus allowing it to take a more proactive approach to troubleshooting. Such automatic evaluations also can help in averting problems, thereby eliminating potential service lapses. As a result, the user can be always guaranteed service, despite the network problems.

• *Security:* ADSL modems perform a considerable amount of handshaking during operation. As a result, it is extremely difficult for the signal to be received by any connection other than the targeted remote unit. As will be explained later in more details in Chapter 8 "Internet Security", security is an important requirement in a telelearning environment. Being able to satisfy this fundamental requirement is a promising feature for ADSL to help increase its adoption rate.

Issues with ADSL

Despite all its advantages, ADSL has a few problem areas. First, similar to ISDN, ADSL users have to be located within a limited radius in order to receive high rate transmissions. The faster the data rate, the shorter the distance must be between the subscriber and the central office. For instance, in order to receive the 9 Mbps rate, customers must be located less than 9000 feet from the central office. This distance is less than that for ISDN (18000 feet). While most customers usually lie within this radius, this condition can be a limiting factor for users in rural areas, for which DLCs or repeaters would be required to enable ADSL access, thus adding to the cost for both telephone companies and users.

In order to provide ADSL connection, phone companies should install ADSL equipment at both ends of the loop connecting the subscriber and the central office. Upgrading thousands of central offices is very time consuming.

Another issue is the lack of standards. The two main ADSL modulation standards existing today, are Carrierless AmPlitude (CAP) and Discrete Multi-Tone (DMT). The main difference lies in the modulation technique used. CAP considers the bandwidth as one big pipe through which as much data as possible is pumped. CAP speeds currently are: 1.5 Mbps downstream and 64 Kbps upstream. DMT, the newer scheme divides the total bandwidth into 256 channels that can handle faster speeds. The advantage is that data is directed away from channels with too much traffic and is sent down clear transmission paths, which in turn, provides high quality connections. DMT transmits at 9 Mbps downstream and 640 Kbps upstream. DMT has a finer grain of rate adaptation and has been endorsed by the American National

Standards Institute. If both technologies are deployed, interoperability problems are bound to exist.

Costs for Students

The price per ADSL line for residential customers is about $60 to $80 per month, which may include Internet access. The ultimate goal of many leading telephone companies is to offer ADSL-based Internet services in the $35-to-$50-per-month range. Based on these prospects, telelearners are very likely to adopt ADSL, by virtue of its high bandwidth at an affordable cost.

Cable Modems

Like telephone companies, cable companies are also at a transition stage from their traditional core business of entertainment video programming, to a position of a full service provider of high speed Internet access, and broad bandwidth applications, at affordable rates. In order to realize these objectives, cable companies have developed the cable modem technology.

A cable modem is a device, similar to the telephone modem, that connects a PC to a hybrid fiber/coax transmission system for high-speed data access (such as to the Internet) via cable TV (CATV) as shown in Figure 6.6.

Figure 6.7, demonstrates the difference between the traditional setting using a regular telephone modem and that using the cable modem.

In the left of the figure, a standard twisted pair is serving the phone and the computer. The right of the figure portrays the cable modem connection, where the cable modem has two connections, one to the television set and the other to the computer (PC).

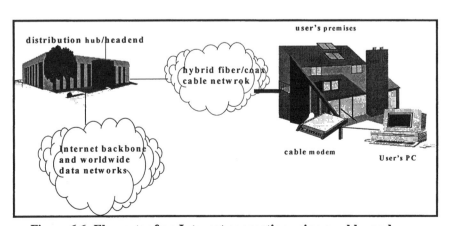

Figure 6.6: Elements of an Internet connection using a cable modem

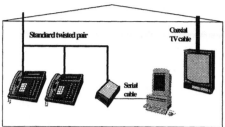

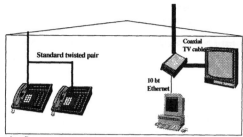

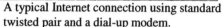

A typical Internet connection using standard twisted pair and a dial-up modem.

An Internet connection using a cable modem

Figure 6.7: Difference in Internet connection using dial-up and cable modems

Similar to telephone modems, cable modems also modulate and demodulate signals. Cable modem operation, however, is much more complicated than that of a telephone modem. A cable modem operates as a modem, a tuner, an encryption/decryption device, a network interface card, in addition to several other functions.

Similar to ADSL, cable modems send and receive data at two different rates with the downstream rate much higher than the upstream rates, as illustrated in Table 6.4.

In the downstream, data is modulated and then placed on a 6 MHz channel, without disturbing the cable television video signals, and is converted to the Ethernet protocol for communication with the computer. There are several modulation schemes, but the most popular are Quadrature Phase Shift Keying or QPSK (up to about 10 Mbps) and Quadrature Amplitude Modulation (QAM) (up to about 30 Mbps).

Modem	Downstream *	Upstream
3Com	30 Mbps	2.6 Mbps
Bay Networks	10 Mbps	10 Mbps
Hewlett Packard	30 Mbps	10 Mbps
Hybrid Net	30 Mbps	3 Mbps
IBM	30 Mbps	512 Kbps
Toshiba	8 Mbps	2 Mbps
Zenith	4 Mbps or 500 Kbps	4 Mbps or 500 Kbps

Source: Cable DataCom News available at http://cabledatacomnews.com/modems.htm

* Modem speeds refer to peak burst rates. Actual throughput is limited by 10BaseT Ethernet connection to the PC and network traffic, as well as the subscriber's PC processing power and software configuration.

Table 6.4: Sample cable modem speeds

In the upstream, or the reverse path, the cable modem takes the Ethernet packets and converts them to analog signals that flow back to the cable company head end. The equipment located at the cable head end, splits off the data signal, converts it to Ethernet packets and directs it to an Internet server. Voice conversations are also stripped off and routed to a local exchange switch if the carrier is also offering a telephony service.

Cable Modems Advantages

Cable modems provide very high-speed data transmissions, with down-stream ranging from 500 Kbps to 30 Mbps, and upstream going from 96 Kbps to 10 Mbps, without interfering with the cable TV services. The high speed transmission rates will promote several broadband and time critical services to users, principally to the telelearning practitioners. Possible applications include:

- High-speed Internet access and high bandwidth applications.
- Audio and video-conferencing via the Internet and the cable, which provides very good opportunity to hold on-line audio/video live lectures and discussions.
- On-line access to educational resources such as educational video servers, local community information and services, and on-line libraries.

At this time, unlimited Internet access rates range between $50 and $80, a price which compares favorably with the rates currently charged by Internet access providers for ADSL service over phone lines.

Several cable companies have already started commercial cable modem deployments. Cable DataCom News publisher Kinetic Strategies Inc., estimates that cable operators were offering two-way cable modem services to 2 million homes in North America in the first quarter of 1997.

Issues with Cable Modems

Because of the cable networks' transmission technique and their original design, cable operators still have to resolve some problems in order to meet the increasing demand for high bandwidth services.

The cable technology originally was designed to support the one way analog transmission of television programs to home. Hence, cable operators need to upgrade their network, so that it supports bi-directional data transfers. Using the Internet, by clicking on web pages hyperlinks, or sending e-mail

Cable co.	Location	Services	Vendors	Notes
Cogeco Cable	Quebec	Commercial Internet services.	Zenith	services also available in Ontario
Rogers Cablesystems	Newmarket, Ontario	Commercial WAVE service offers unlimited Internet access for C$39.95/month	Zenith	More than 800 paying subscribers, approx. 5% penetration of basic cable subs in suburban Toronto
Rogers Cablesystems	London and North York, Ontario.	Commercial WAVE service offers unlimited Internet access for C$55/month	Zenith	Rogers has also launched WAVE in Brampton, Hamilton, Ottawa and Vancouver
Shaw Communications	Calgary and Toronto.	Commercial WAVE service offers unlimited Internet access for C$55/month	Motorola	WAVE service offered under Canadian MSO alliance
Videotron	Montreal and Alberta.	Commercial launch of high-speed Internet service	Motorola	Montreal deployment includes InfiniT content service.

Source: http://cabledatacomnews.com/trials.htm

Table 6.5: Cable modem service providers in Canada

messages, requires the system to send the user's data request through the cable infrastructure and to receive the information that's sent back. To become interactive, cable operators must allocate spectrum on the cable for upstream signals.

Right now, several cable companies are upgrading their networks into a hybrid digital and analog systems, by transforming cable systems into hybrid fiber-coax or HFC networks. Systems are currently being designed with fiber running out to nodes serving 500 and 2,000 homes. Table 6.5 lists the different services in Canada.

One other issue is that cable modems on the same node share bandwidth, which means that congestion is created when too many people are on-line simultaneously. By way of illustration, if two telelearners living in the same neighborhood are downloading large graphic or multimedia files at the same time, they can use up a significant portion of the shared bandwidth, and therefore slow each other's access. Cable operators solve this problem by engineering the network so as to limit the number of users sharing any given cable modem. However, shared access remains a fundamental difference between cable modems and ADSL, which is a dedicated access technology.

As high bandwidth real time applications such as video-conferencing via the Internet become more commonplace for telelearning, guaranteed band-width becomes very important. With shared cable modem access, guaranteed bandwidth will likely be offered as a premium service. This means that only those who are willing to pay more will be guaranteed bandwidth.

In order to create an apparent faster network, and to eliminate Internet bottlenecks, many of the foremost cable companies in the cable modem field, are planning to store or "cache" the frequently requested web sites and Usenet groups on a local server. The problem which might arise in this case, is when a user requests a file which does not reside on the headend server. Cable operators, however are currently working on solving this problem by expanding their server capacity.

Upstream, data may be transmitted via a low frequency band that hasn't previously been used. This can create a "noisy" environment for cable modems, created by interference from HAM and CB radios and impulse noise from home appliances. Additionally, interference can be easily introduced in the home, due to loose connectors or poor cabling. Moreover, the tree and branch structure of cable networks tends to amplify the noise as the signals travel upstream. On account of this problem, most manufacturers will use QPSK or a similar modulation scheme in the upstream direction, as it is more powerful than higher order modulation techniques in a noisy environment. The drawback is that QPSK is "slower" than QAM.

Cable companies entering the Internet market need to recruit people with a high level of technical expertise and a thorough understanding of TCP/IP networking. In order to manage the Internet traffic, cable operators will have to set up routers and servers at the head end and at strategic places around the cable system.

Another location issue, which can be very costly to solve is when the student's PC isn't near the TV or any cable plugs. In order to have Internet access via cable, the cable company will need to rewire the user's house and link the computer to the cable system, which can add to the cost.

At this time, where the cable modem use is limited to Internet access, having an asymmetric service, with a much higher bandwidth allocated for downstream channel than the upstream is acceptable. Most of the common Internet applications today, tend to be asymmetric in nature. Downloading Web files, browsing the Internet resources and reading newsgroups send more data towards the user than to the network. On the other hand, uploads are generally limited to Mouse clicks (URL requests) and e-mail messages, which are not bandwidth intensive. This situation however, is changing as symmetric bandwidth applications are being used. Within a telelearning environment, real time applications such as video and audio conferencing, and multimedia exchanges are very essential for an effective on-line delivery

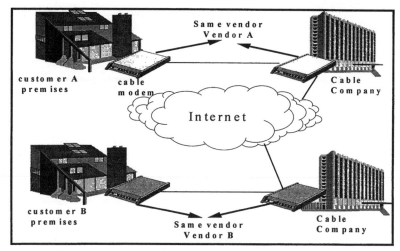

Figure 6.8: Required use of same vendor equipment at the cable company and the customer premises.

of educational material. This is also the case with ADSL. In order to get a symmetric bandwidth of 640 Kbps for a multimedia conference, a top of the line ADSL service with 6-9 Mbps downstream is required. Versions of ADSL with lower downstream bandwidth also have a lower symmetric bandwidth capability.

One other concern regarding cable modems is user training. In order to ensure efficient use of the new tools, user training is essential. The fact that some leading ISPs have stopped providing inexpensive Internet access, due to the demanding customer service requirements and dealing with inexperienced users, implies that extensive training and support is required. Cable modem advocates look upon this issue as a one-time requirement, and do not consider it as a major issue.

Until recently there has been a lack of standards for cable modems. Each manufacturer has been using a different data-transmission specification, resulting in problems of incompatibility. If students decide to move to another city, they will need a new cable modem from the local cable operator, which represents extra costs. As illustrated in Figure 6.8.

Costs for Students

With cable modem services becoming more commercially available, several cable operators have been trying to bring access charges down to encourage subscribers to use the technology by offering high speed data service packages, much like they do for basic television service. At this time, charges vary between $40 and $60 per month for an Internet service package, which includes software, unlimited Internet access, specialized content and

Cost element	cost
Cable modem	$500
Installation cost *	$50
Initial costs	$550
Access service	$30
Monthly cost s	$30

* Assuming the user has an installed cable and the PC is already configured for Ethernet.

Table 6.6: Summary of costs of an ADSL connection

a cable modem.

The costs involved with using a cable modem comprise the following:

• *Cable modem*: at this time (1996-1997), manufacturers are selling cable modem at around $500. Prices are expected to drop to $200 for standardized products as sales volumes expand.
• *Access Service:* Cable modems are not initially sold in retail computer distribution channels. Instead, users lease the modems from the cable company much as they do with cable converter boxes today. Estimates range form $20 to $50 per month for unlimited access time.
• *Installation:* Cable companies typically charge between $50 and $150 for installation fees. The charge depends on whether the user's PC is configured for Ethernet or not and whether the home already has cable installed.

Table 6.6 summarizes the expenses of accessing the Internet using a cable modem.

Comparative Analysis of all Internet Access Options for Telelearning Student via the Internet

A comparison of the access options described above is given in Table 6.7. Table 6.8 displays sample times for transferring data using existing and emerging technologies.

By comparing the different technologies, it appears that many on-line students are very likely to continue using the 28.8 Kbps modems for the near term future. As standards emerge for the 56 Kbps modems, it is anticipated that on-line students and instructors would shift to these faster tools. Since 56 Kbps modems transmission rate is close to single channel ISDN (64 Kbps),

	Possible services	speed upload/ download	Efficiency in a telelearning environment	Pros	Cons
Dial- in modems	Asynchronous and real time text based communication, audio conferences. Text based file exchanges.	14.4-33 Kbps/ 14.4-33 Kbps	Very low for multimedia applications - Acceptable for asynchron-ous and low bandwidth real time interactions.	Affordable and widely available Permits several applications: (e-mail, text based conferencing, asynchronous multimedia communication)	Very slow.
56 Kbps modem	High speed downloads. Video and audio conferencing	33 Kbps /56 Kbps	Good	Acceptable price, Does not need additional equipment. More convenient and lower cost than ISDN.	Lacks standards
ISDN	Fast downloads and uploads of large files. Audio and video-conferences.	56-128 Kbps/56 - 128 Kbps.	Good-very good	Wide availability in Europe; Mature technology and products.	Still not ubiquitous. Some services are costly. Hard to configure
ADSL	Faster downloads and uploads than ISDN. Audio and video-conferences. More effective application of high bandwidth technologies	16-640 Kbps/ 1.5-9 Mbps	Very good	Uses existing infrastructure Permits 24hr on-line access.	Won't be ubiquitous in the near term. More expensive than ISDN. Two competing standards
Cable modems	Audio and video-conferences. High speed uploads and downloads of multimedia files.	99.6 Kbps-10 Mbps /50 Kbps-30 Mbps.	Very good	Good price performance ratio. Recently standardized.	Immature technology, and products. Won't be widely available in the near term. Bandwidth shared with other users.

* Possible services for all technologies other than dial in modems, include those which are extra to the basic dial in modems possible applications.

Table : 6.7 Comparison of Internet access options

	File size (Mbit)	Modem (14.4 Kbps)	ISDN (128 Kbps)	ADSL (1.5 Mbps)	Cable modem (4 Mbps)
Simple image	2	2.3 min.	15.6 sec	1.3 sec	0.5 sec
Complex image	16	18.5 min.	2.1 min.	10.7 sec	4 sec
Animation or video	72	1.4 hr	9.37 min.	48 sec	18 sec

Table 6.8 : Sample transfer times of high speed technologies

and is more convenient and lower cost, competition is expected to arise, and the pace of ISDN deployment may slow down. Since most of the telelearning practitioners are price-sensitive customers, 56 Kbps modems might be more popular among telelearners than ISDN.

As high bandwidth requirements for Internet-based telelearning operations increase to include more video-conferencing and multimedia files transfer, ADSL and cable modem technologies are likely to become more widely used, in cities where carriers offer these services.

Tuition Fees

There are still no common rules for setting on-line courses tuition fees. With the increasing competition between on-line education providers, it is likely that tuition fees would drop. However, a niche market with high tuition fees at high quality virtual institutions might also emerge. For the time being, fees range between two extremes. Except in a few cases, many on-line academic institutions do not provide any justification or breakdown of their fees. Tuition fees however, do not always reflect the value of the program and the level and competency of the teaching staff, which might lead in some cases to costly and unfavorable results for telelearners.

Also, the lack of clear rules about setting tuition fees can be a discriminating factor against students who can't afford paying high tuition fees, but wish to receive a high quality education. Moreover, the international aspect of on-line courses, and the different life standards across the world are two main elements which should be considered when setting on-line programs tuition fees, since high prices can deprive those in countries with low standards of living from taking expensive courses.

CyberHigh, a virtual high school, offers credit courses for free and provides its students with the computer resources. The only charge a CyberHigh student has to pay is a CDN$100 registration fee, which breaks down to three parts:

- CDN$50 for textbook rental. This is non-refundable to compensate for the costs of wear and tear of books.
- CDN$50 for computer maintenance and lease, since in order for the student's insurance company to cover the computer on their home insurance, it may need to be a leased item. This fee also pays for the computer at the end of the year.

Cost element	($US)
CALCampus Student Admission	45
High School Diploma On-line Program Application:	20
Written Communication	49
Consumer Mathematics	49
Reading Comprehension	49
American History	49
Government & Voter Responsibility	49
Law & Society	49
Graduation, Transcript, and American Academy Diploma	124
Total	483

Table 6.9 : Breakdown of CALCampus High School On-line Diploma fees.

Unlike CyberHigh, CyberEd, an on-line virtual university, charges for both its credit and non-credit courses. CyberEd students would have to pay $437 for a graduate 3-credit course, $365 for an undergraduate three-credit course, and $135 for a non-credit course. These fees include a $68 processing fee for credit courses, and $10 for non-credit courses.

CALCampus, a service of the Computer Assisted Learning Center (CALC), is a virtual learning center offering courses to adults, high school and college students. According to Ms. Morabito, CALCampus director, the institution has "...set...prices low in order to allow everyone to participate, not just the wealthy". She adds that "In the US, (CALCampus) prices would be comparable to a community adult education center". Ms Morabito explains that CALCampus tuition fees are low because of its low operational costs, besides the low compensation rate of its instructors.

Table 6.9 provides a breakdown of the tuition fees of its CALCampus High School On-line Diploma. Charges for the required courses are the same as when the same course is taken separately.

An on-line course does not necessarily cost less than an on-campus course. While telelearning via the Internet is cost effective in terms of reaching a wider range of students, and saving on buildings, it brings new costs not associated with traditional face to face courses. These costs include, among many others:

• The additional staff required for computer support and training of instructors and students.

• Time intensive development of on-line courses.
• Extra need for assistance for handling assignments and tutorials when the class size is large.
• Copyright expenses for using copyrighted material.

An Internet board of education might solve this issue. The role of this "International board of education" would be to set criteria of setting tuition fees to all Internet courses. This can depend on the level of the course, type of the degree, the number of hours needed to finish the course, security costs and copyright charges. The charges however, should be within a certain range, which should be considered to be affordable by most international students. If not, the benefits of worldwide access to high quality education might not be realized, since high tuition fees would be a discriminating factor against a certain number of students.

Setting a clear set of rules determining Internet on-line courses fees would provide students with a clear idea about the different elements of the tuition they are paying and help them evaluate the different available courses.

Other Costs

These costs can include the following:

• Costs of textbooks and other required studying materials, provided by the instructor, from time to time. Print material costs, however can be also included in the tuition fees.
• With the increasing digitization of learning material, and the progression towards solving Internet material copyright issues, students will have more flexible access to course material. A new cost element however, is likely to arise: the cost of accessing and using copyrighted material. This cost can be applied in many ways such as:
—When requesting the material from the supplier, via Internet forms or using the traditional payment methods for better security, or
—By paying for a secret key or a password which allows the user to access the material whenever needed.

At this time, copyright charges are not yet applied, and therefore no clear costing criteria have been set. It is expected though, that costs might be proportional to hard copies, such as in the case of books. Clear guidelines should be developed for pricing files with multiple sections of different copyrighted materials, in order to prevent any infringements.

- Charges for accessing the institution's internal campus Web site and courses material.
- Charges for using security tools such as passwords and encryption keys.
- ISP charges: today, with the increased competition between ISPs, users are offered several attractive packages at very low rates. As high speed Internet access technologies become more common, charges based on the amount of connection time would not be significant for ISPs. Instead, they might set charges, which are based on the amount of data sent and received. This might initially, increase costs for students using high bandwidth applications such as video-conferencing and downloading large multimedia large files.

Chapter 7

■

Institution Related Costs

Most of the costs for partially and totally on-line institutions are the same. Hybrid organizations, which will be offering both conventional and on-line programs, or those which have replaced some of their conventional courses with Internet-based ones, are very likely to save on a certain number of cost elements, such as facilities, staff, and buildings maintenance. Some of the main cost savings elements are examined under the section "Savings for partially on-line institutions." On the other hand, offering courses on-line will also bring in a new set of cost elements, such as Web site construction, and on-line technical support. Other costs will be discussed in more detail under the section, "Costs of establishing an Internet-based academic institution.

Costs which have been always incurred by partially on-line institutions will not be considered. These include costs such as computer labs, terminals, computer staff salaries, maintenance and accommodations costs.

Savings for Partially On-line Institutions

Many academic institutions today are starting to offer more Internet-based courses and programs as a solution to their shrinking budget and the lower enrollment rates. At the same time, offering courses on-line can result in savings at many levels. Some of the cost elements where savings are likely to be realized include:

- *Facilities:* institutions will be saving on facilities and maintenance, such as classrooms, offices, computer labs, facilities maintenance, heat, janitorial services, which are ongoing costs and increasing as the number of students increase.
- *Learning material expenses*: the easy digitization and the low costs of on-line publishing significantly reduces learning material costs. For instance,

instructors at the VOU (Virtual On-line University), CALCampus and CyberEd write their own hypertext books on-line, which can later browsed by students for free.

• *Instructors' expenses:* At CALCampus for instance, the instructors income is only from the tuition fees. Many of them are also teaching in conventional classes. Therefore, they are not totally financially dependent on on-line courses. Some instructors are paid extra for when remote students are added to a conventional class. However the amount of this payment varies greatly from one institution to another. Training courses are available for instructors to learn the specifics of teaching in an on-line environment, so that training costs may be a one time cost to the instituion.

• *Internet access:* Upgrading the Internet access to a higher speed line may be required, particularly in case the institution decides to deliver its program using broad bandwidth live applications such as interactive video-conferencing. The benefit of this upgrade will be shared by telelearners taking the course on-line. The benefits of the upgrade, however, might not be fully appreciated in case the on-line students have low speed connections and can only receive low bandwidth applications such text, audio and asynchronous multimedia file retrieval.

Costs of Establishing a Virtual Internet-based Academic Institution

The main costs incurred when a program is launched on-line via the Internet are:

• Cost of planning and preparing the strategy and policies.
• Cost of constructing a web site.
• Cost of upgrading and developing the on-line programs.
• Teacher, tutors and support staff training.
• Computer software support staff costs.
• Maintenance and upgrade costs of computer servers as new technologies are developed.
• Instructors and tutors' compensation costs.

Planning and Strategy Design Costs

The costs of planning and designing the institution's strategy are mainly time costs. With the increased competition in the on-line education field, the institution's staff should spend a considerable amount of time on designing a comprehensive and sound strategy. Both administrative staff as well as instructors should be actively involved in the design process. The plan should encompass elements such as: administration, pedagogy, finance, and marketing.

The following are some of the important activities which should be accomplished when designing the strategy:

- Formulate the institution's mission statement, the long term goals as well as the medium and short term objectives. These are very important prerequuisites for any further action in order to ensure conformity and consistency in everybody's objectives and work plans.
- Prepare a strategy plan for the server's operations. The plan should include all elements such as financial, marketing and long term strategies for raising funding resources and providing server users such as instructors and students with the appropriate services. For instance the team should decide on points such as:

The type of environment for interaction:

- Asynchronous vs. synchronous,
- Real time text based only such as IRC, text based with hypermedia such as MUD and MOO environments, Web conferencing, or real time video-conferencing using CUSeeMe for instance.

1. Level of security: use passwords, encryption using public and/or private keys, digital signatures, etc.
2. Applications to support on-line interaction: Java, VRML, Shockwave, etc.
3. Features to be included: tables, Web search engines, mailing list service, database management, animation, institution's logo and unique graphics, scanned images (color & greyscale), periodic updating and maintenance.
4. Payment procedures: on-line vs. traditional methods such as fax, regular mail and phone.
5. If payments will be made on-line, then an on-line payment system and an on-line order processing system should be designed.
6. Plans for further uses of the server as a cash generator: by offering test web spaces, for instance, or leasing out space for clients to have their own web pages.

• Form the team of people who will be working on the institution's server and Web pages maintenance and upgrades, and train them by an Internet specialist. To cite an instance, a programmer can be needed for the server programming and the integration of computer applications such as Java and VRML, while a graphic artist is responsible of the Web page design.

• Setting staff and instructors' training schedules for mastering the on-line environment.

• For a partially on-line institution, it is assumed that they already have an Internet connection. New, totally on-line institutions would have to carry out the following steps:

—Choose the line connection technology to access the Internet. Depending on their budgets and requirements, staff should make their decision while taking into consideration future operations, such as heavy multimedia real time applications. For partially on-line institutions, as mentioned earlier, upgrades to the line might be required, especially when a heavy network traffic is anticipated.

—Acquire the necessary assistant devices for running the server. These include:

—A router incorporating a CSU/DSU, costing in the range of $2000 to $3000.

—Adapter cards for each computer terminal on the LAN (about $50/card)

—A hub connecting terminals to the server. Depending on their speed hub interface prices can range between $100 (10 Mbps interfaces) up to $1000 (100 Mbps interfaces).

These are some of the principal elements which should be determined before starting the program on-line. Once all of the strategy requirements are satisfied and final decisions are made, the program can then be launched. Some on-line institutions, such as CyberHigh for instance, initiated the program for an experimental period. Based on the students and the faculty feedback, necessary changes and improvements are supplemented, after which a final work plan is set and the program is then introduced to the open on-line telelearners community.

It is very important to note, also, that the strategy should be periodically reviewed and updated in order to ensure that all the activities are being accurately implemented and that all objectives are being achieved. In case the institution has a high speed access, faculty meetings could be held live on-line, in order to save on travel and time costs. On-line timely meetings perfectly suit crisis management situations, and add flexibility to staff operations, which in turn can significantly increase the institution's efficiency and productivity.

Web Site Construction Costs

Any virtual or partially on-line university operating via the Internet counts on a large number of students and interested Internet users to access its site. Through a Web site, the institution can recruit students and faculty, provide campus wide information and provide research opportunities and access to wide information resources for insiders as well as outsiders. The way a Web page is designed can be a very powerful tool, which can be used to compete with other competent on-line institutions, especially if they are offering the same program.

Paying for a Web server is not a very costly element for institutions. For hybrid institutions, maintaining and running the Web server can be done by students and instructors from the institution's computer department, and running the Web site can be even made part of the computer course curriculum. Virtual institutions, on the other hand, might need to hire specialized technicians.

The steps involved in a site construction involve:

1. *Setting up a test page:* It is recommended to set up a test page before establishing the official site. The institution can use someone else's server to be its test bed. Test Web pages can be put up for less than $500 a year through hosting services. Besides housing the institution's Web documents, the additional options which come with the hosting service package can help the institution in establishing itself in the Internet community. One such important service is the super high-end HTML self-store option, which helps making credit transactions. This option can be helpful to settle tuition payments of the first students who will be joining the institution.

2. *Hiring a Web specialist or Internet consultant:* The Web specialist role is very critical, since pitfalls due to inappropriate designs can be very costly, and can affect the institution's long term plan. The very basic role of an Internet consultant is to set up the server. However, consultants can be hired for a longer term to assist in managing the server building process, and to train those who will be responsible of the server maintenance, later. Short term Web specialist fees range between $60 and $150 per hour, depending on the region where they are operating. While long term or general consultants' fees can be anywhere between $750 to $2000 per day depend-

Site construction cost element	Notes
Test page web hosting Web server	$200 setup +$50/month until the site is transferred to the institution's web server.
Internet consultant or Web specialist	$60 to $150/hour depending on the region. Charges cover the institution and/or instructors web pages design.
Domain name registration	$100 for the domain name + $50 annual fee

Table 7.1: Site construction costs

ing primarily on the consultant's expertise.

3. *Choosing and registering a domain name for the server with InterNIC.* InterNIC charges $100 per domain plus a $50 annual fee.

4. *Deciding on the hardware to be used for running the server:* At this time, Windows NT Internet information sever offers many Internet ready applications, and makes it an economical solution for running servers.

Table 7.1 summarizes the different site construction costs:

Cost of Upgrading and Developing the On-line Programs

Based on a discussion held over the DEOS-L mailing list, instructors who plan to give an on-line course are in some cases provided with a grant to hire an assistant to help them in the preparation of the on-line courses. In other cases, instructors willing to offer an on-line course receive a bonus for the extra time they spend on the development. Some participants mentioned that developing an on-line course for the first time is a similar time commitment to starting a course from scratch and includes designing classes, reference material, Web pages, searching and integrating the required links, etc. Subsequent updates, however, are not as time consuming.

Teacher, Tutors and Support Staff Training

Training sessions for teachers, tutors and support staff should be done on a periodic basis, especially with the rapid technological developments in the Internet field. With virtual educational institutions providing international education, it is very likely that the teaching staff would be scattered in different parts of the world. Grouping all the staff in one location to be trained, would therefore represent an exorbitant cost. On-line training would be the most cost efficient, highly flexible and productive method to ensure that all the staff are receiving the same training, and that they are always kept up to date with any changes. This type of training is in itself a telelearning application.

One other cost, which cannot be avoided is the trainers' charges. Trainers' expenses usually depend on their expertise, experience and number of training hours.

Computer Software Support Staff Costs

Computer software staff should always be available on-line in order to provide support for instructors and students while they are using computing resources. They usually have an e-mail address on the institution's main Web page where they can be contacted whenever necessary.

Maintenance and Upgrade Costs of Computer Servers and Other Hardware

These costs can be very high especially when the server needs to be changed. However, these costs are not incurred as frequently as upgrade costs. Hardware upgrades and improvements can be very frequent and at no fixed schedule, on account of the rapid technological advances. Maintenance costs, therefore, can vary widely form one period to another, depending on the number of upgrades needed.

Instructors and Tutors' Compensation Costs

There are no exact guidelines for how payments of on-line instructors should be made. For instance they can depend on the number of students taking the course, the number of on-line hours, the number of courses they give, etc.

Table 7.2 summarizes the different costs and their nature: periodic, one time costs.

Establishing a Business Case

It is not always possible to establish a business case for setting up a virtual educational institution since many of the cost elements are difficult to

Cost element	Cost nature
Cost of strategy planning	big initial time investment shorter periodic review sessions
Cost of the web site construction Test page web hosting	initial one time setup cost periodic monthly costs until the site is transferred to the institution's web server.
Web server	one time cost
Internet consultant or Web specialist	one time cost
Domain name registration	one time cost for domain name registration + periodic annual fee
Cost of developing on-line programs	one time cost
Teacher, tutors & support staff training	periodic
Computer software support staff costs	periodic
Maintenance and computing resources upgrades	periodic
Instructors and tutors' compensation costs	periodic

Table 7.2: Summary of institution related costs

quantify. In order to identify the issues involved we interviewed several organizations, including virtual institutions such as CALCampus, CyberEd, CyberHigh, Virtual On-line University and Diversity University, University of Colorado On-line, and others which are partially on-line, such as CSU, the Ontario Institute of Studies in Education and the Canadian Union of Public Employees. The main conclusion was that:

For totally on-line institutions, most of the costs are start up costs and are incurred once. On-going costs such as server maintenance and instructors' fees, on the other hand, are in most cases much lower than those of conventional institutions. For instance, in CALCampus costs include: computer hardware that the administrative staff use, the Internet connection and server software. Instructors at CALCampus are part-timers, and are paid on a per student basis from the income from the students' fees. According to CALCampus' director: "(CALCampus) teachers do not make lot of money. They are teaching because they love to teach, they enjoy the on-line medium, and they enjoy their students...Our benefits are intangible, such as satisfaction from a job well done." There are no related training costs, as it is the institution's teachers and the director herself who train new instructors.

At other institutions such as CyberEd, which is a department of the University of Massachusetts, Dartmouth, instructors teach both on-line and conventional classes. Those teaching credit courses are compensated exactly the same as they are for teaching in a face to face UMass course. Instructors teaching non-credit courses, on the other hand, are paid on a per-student basis, with the number of students not exceeding 25 in any CyberEd class. According to CyberEd's coordinator, it is difficult to assess the costs related to operating CyberEd, since many of the faculty and administrative staff are continuously contributing to upgrade CyberEd's environment from their own time. Moreover, many of CyberEd's developments are used to supplement UMass' conventional classes.

At Central State University On-line Programs Department, John M. Anderson, the department's vice president points that "(CSU) maintains a pool of highly competent adjunct professors whom (they) can hire at a rate which doesn't include normal perks supplied for full-time professors," which means that the institution saves considerably on the instructors' costs.

With regard to hybrid institutions, i.e. those offering both conventional and on-line courses, there are no costs related to equipment, facilities or Internet connection, since these resources are being shared between the different network's applications. As a result, adding one or a set of on-line courses won't add any extra costs.

Concerning the instructors' costs, payment policies differ from one institution to another. In many cases, instructors are not paid any extra for the on-line course, especially when they are already offering the same course within the conventional settings, i.e. the course is offered both for on campus and on-line students. In other cases, an instructor is provided with a grant to hire an assistant for the process of transferring the course on-line. Based on a DEOS-L discussion concerning this issue, many instructors transferred their courses on-line using their own time and did not receive any extra compensation for that. In other cases, especially when the course is offered just on-line, instructors are paid on a per student basis or they are paid in the same way as other professors offering a face to face to course. It is important to note, though, that many instructors, especially those offering individual non-credit courses, are giving on-line courses in order to improve their computer literacy, and/or to experiment with Internet tools and their effectiveness in delivering education. Many others are just doing it for the sake of teaching and in order to provide knowledge for those who might not be able to acquire it otherwise. This is why it is very common that on-line instructors are either part-timers receiving minimum compensation, or are just offering the course for free.

Conclusion

Setting and taking part in an Internet based telelearning program is a very cost effective alternative to face-to-face learning, both for the educational institution's administrative and pedagogic staff, as well as for students.

Declining computer equipment prices, along with the increased availability of affordable Internet access options are important factors for students when taking an on-line course. Tuition fees, however, which vary considerably between institutions, can raise their bill considerably, especially since some virtual institutions are charging the same fees as their on campus students. This may be because many students prefer telelearning via the Internet mainly because of the flexibility it offers. Increasing competition however, might bring down this cost element.

When it comes to institutions, it is certainly a cost effective alternative for delivering education, making savings on costs such as buildings expenses, especially with the shrinking budgets and the reduced government funding. Even start up costs, such as web site construction and equipment expenses, are one time costs and are also continuously dropping in prices. Costs such as training, computer maintenance and compensation need to be well managed, for instance by holding training sessions via the Internet instead of bringing in all trainees to a common site, using students for computer maintenance and paying a minimal honorarium for instructors.

Part IV

■

Issues With Telelearning via the Internet

Despite all its numerous benefits, and like any other technology expanding at an rapid pace, the Internet still has several issues, which should be resolved soon, if most of the expectations of a universal, effective and successful telelearning environment are to be realized. Fortunately, most of these issues have been recognized and are being tackled.

We focus in this section on issues which can significantly affect an Internet-based telelearning setting, and can influence the value of its delivered material. The issues we examine comprise security and privacy, which are discussed in Chapter 8, and are considered to be among the primary discouraging factors for some academic institutions to go on-line, as was discussed in Part 2, such as the case of Harvard and Stanford Universities.

Next, we examine in Chapter 9, some prominent policy issues, which include electronic documents copyright, accreditation of virtual academic institutions, on-line academic fraud and evaluation of the Web site's content and creator.

In each chapter, a discussion is first provided about how the problem relates to Internet-based telelearning. Next, some of the solutions to solve these issues are suggested.

.

Chapter 8

■

Internet Security

Security management over the Internet is a growing challenge, primarily because of the open hierarchy of this universal network, and the expanding connectivity, which can get easily out of control. Some people contend that the capabilities of security products are still lagging behind those of other Internet products. If the promise of a secure environment is to be fully realized, it is important to assure users that the information they transmit is not susceptible to fraud, copying, damaging or any other misuse.

In this chapter, the emphasis is mainly on network technical security. Other security related issues such as academic fraud, copyright, accreditation and evaluation of the Web site's content, were classified under policy issues and will be discussed later in Chapter 9.

When operating within a telelearning environment via the Internet, security becomes a very fundamental requirement, especially in certain cases, such as:

• Sharing sensitive information in group work and projects. This can be either in text, audio, or even video format.
• Carrying on lectures and class discussions for registered students only.
• Submission of tests and assignments.
• Making on-line tests and quizzes.
• On-line tuition fees and other charges payments.

In order to ensure an effective safe, private and secure environment, Internet-based telelearning academic organizations should satisfy the following elements of security:

Access control: ensuring that the course materials are only accessible to registered students, and authorized faculty. This would limit access to the institution's Web server and protect internal information from outsiders.

Authentication: ensuring that the senders of on-line documents at the other end of the session are really who they claim to be. When students take on-line exams, for instance, teachers need to be sure that the exam papers really do come from their students. This requirement can be difficult to satisfy, especially in case passwords are used as a security measure. Any one who intentionally or unintentionally gains access to the password can use it pretending that it is the password's owner who is sending the message. This is why more sophisticated and safer methods should be used as will be discussed in the coming sections.

Integrity: assuring that the received information is the same as when it was sent and that no modifications were introduced. This is an essential requirement for on-line classes, especially during exams and sending multi-media documents, which should not be altered.

Accountability: assuring that any transaction that takes place between the two or multiple ends of a session can be proved to have taken place. When students pay their fees, both the school administration and students should agree that the exchange took place. Also, when telelearners receive their diploma from their on-line institutions to use it later to find employment, they will need to be able to prove that it was really signed by the dean (authentication) and that they really received it from the academic institution (accountability).

Privacy: That is assuring that any sensitive information is kept private, and that is not visible to eavesdroppers. This requirement is very important while receiving exam papers, where information should be protected from cheating and alterations during transmission.

Security over the Web

Putting a WWW server for a course or a virtual academic institution over the Internet implies inviting telelearners and other interested Internet users to access the server, browse information and ask questions. Exposure of the institution's database and internal information resources, however, should be limited to certain authorized individuals, such as registered students and staff. In order to protect the institution's server from outside attacks and eavesdroppers, sound and reliable security administration and firewalls should be implemented.

The nature of the Web makes it very vulnerable to hackers' attacks. The WWW consists of two superimposed networks: a data communication network, which is the Internet, and an application layer network. The data communication network is a collection of several networks linked by routing networks. The distributed structure of this network increases risks of eavesdropping on transmitted information. The application layer network consists of servers and clients scattered around the Internet, exchanging HTTP files. HTTP files can imbed different types of data (graphics, sound, text, etc.). On the browser, each data type is associated with a presentation program called a viewer. These programs are often large and complex, which increases the risk of spreading bugs and viruses. Moreover, some of the file formats, such as Postscript, contain some programmability. As a result, a hacker can use these features to execute programs or to install data on the client machine.

For each layer some mechanisms have been developed in order to provide a safe and secure environment.

Security at the Application Layer

In the application layer, the following two mechanisms are being applied:

The WWW basic security mechanism:
This mechanism is also referred to as basic authentication. Basic authentication is a system that uses IDs and passwords to apply access control to documents and files in a server. Under this mechanism, a client can only access a server if it provides a valid ID and password. The server, therefore, can identify who the client user is by means of the provided information. Almost all virtual telelearning institutions operating using different Internet tools, such as IRC, MUDs, MOOs or Web conferencing, use passwords as a means of limiting access to their information resources and servers. To illustrate, on-line institutions such as CyberEd, Diversity University, and CyberHigh, use passwords to limit open public access to their lectures sessions. On the other hand, main home pages, which include general information about the organization, contact addresses, public areas access such as student lounges and information desks are open for public access.

Even though basic authentication is widely use by almost all Internet conferencing applications, such as Web conferencing, MUDs and MOOs, it is not a reliable security mechanism to ensure user authentication. The following cases prove the vulnerability of basic authentication:

• Students can deliberately give their passwords to another person.
• Someone might guess the password, and use it to access private areas.
• Someone might be using a password without the knowledge of its owner.
• Someone might catch the ID between the client and the server.

The three first problems are very common with any password system, even non Internet-based ones. Strict security rules and better user education can limit these problems, but are very unlikely to eliminate them. The last case, for instance, depends on the level of protection given to messages by the HTTP protocol. The stateless nature of this protocol does not allow the server to retain knowledge about the client once the document is served. Consequently, the client has to provide the password every time a document is needed, in which case hackers are offered more chances to capture the password. Several browsers are circumventing this problem today, by sending the ID and password in all subsequent requests for the same server. Even though this method reduces the number of messages sent, it still allows hackers setting up a listening point to a busy server to capture a stream of passwords.

The real solution for the fragility of basic authentication is to use encryption-based mechanisms.

Encryption-based mechanisms:
These systems provide various levels of security including: authentication, integrity, accountability and privacy, by applying cryptography to the connection. Several cryptography protocols, with different objectives, have been developed for securing the Web. Although none of these protocols is a complete standard some are widely used. Two of the most popular protocols are Secure Socket Layer protocol (SSL), which is being used by Netscape Navigator, and the Secure Hypertext Transfer Protocol (S-HTTP). Both protocols use a combination of several cryptographic techniques in order to satisfy most of the security objectives.

The following section describes the three common cryptographic techniques used by these protocols to perform their tasks, which are symmetric-key encryption, public-key encryption as secure hash functions which are used primarily for digital signatures.

Symmetric-key encryption

Symmetric-key encryption or secret key encryption is a cryptographic technique where the two parties share a secret key. Data are encrypted and decrypted using the same key. As shown in figure 8.1 below, the sender encrypts data using the key. Once transmitted, the receiver should use the same key to interpret the message.

The main problem with secret key cryptography is getting the sender and the receiver to agree on the secret key safely, without anyone else finding out. If they are in separate physical locations, as is the case for telelearning class members, they must use a trusted courier, or a phone system, or some other transmission medium, to prevent the disclosure of the secret key being communicated. By overhearing or intercepting the key in transit, an eavesdropper can later use the key to read, modify, and reconstruct all messages encrypted or authenticated with that key.

Key management, which includes the generation, transmission and storage of keys, is very critical in an open system such as Internet-based telelearning settings. Because all keys in a secret-key crypto-system must remain secret, secret-key cryptography often has difficulty providing safe key management. Having the instructor managing the keys helps minimizing security risks, since they will be under the supervision of a trusted high-authority. We should note though that for telelearning settings, public-key cryptography system would be more suitable as will be discussed under the section, Public-key cryptography.

Two of the commonly used symmetric-key algorithms are: DES and IDEA.

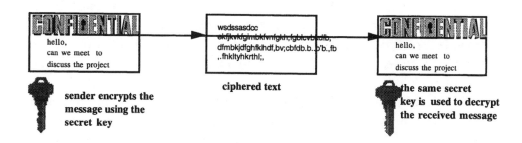

Figure 8.1: Symmetric key encryption stages

- DES, standing for Data Encryption Standard, is a standardized algorithm and is being used worldwide, especially in the financial industry and by several governments. Despite its popularity, its short 56-bits key feature, makes it fairly easy to break with modern computers or special hardware. New variants of DES- such as Triple DES or 3DES, which uses DES three times with different unrelated keys-are providing a higher level of security.
- IDEA (International Data Encryption Algorithm) is another symmetric key algorithm which is also implemented worldwide especially in Europe. IDEA uses a 128-bit key, and is generally considered to be very secure.

Public-key encryption

This encryption system was introduced in order to solve symmetric-key management problems. Instead of having one shared key, users have a pair of keys: a private key, known only by its user, and a public key made publicly available. Each person's public key is known by all other users, while the private key is kept secret.

This technique provides both: privacy and authentication.

Privacy/Confidentialty

Since the information can be only interpreted by the private key, users do not need anymore to share any private information over different communication media, which can be aimed to spying. All message interchanges only involve public keys, which are associated with their owners in a trusted (or authenticated) way, such as a directory. When a user sends a confidential message, he/she encrypts it using the recipient's public key. Once received, the message can only be decrypted using the recipient's secret key.

Authentication

This is achieved by having the message signed electronically by the sender's digital signature. Compared to a handwritten signature, a digital signature asserts the contents of a message, as well as the identity of the user. Digital signatures will be described in more details under secure hash functions.

Figure 8.2 illustrates the different steps of public-key encryption. Public-key encryption provides its users with several advantages over symmetric-key cryptography. The primary advantage is increased security and convenience, by eliminating the need of private exchanges of secret keys.

One example of the most commonly used public-key algorithms is RSA

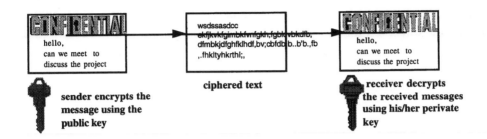

hello,
can we meet to
discuss the project

wsdssasdcc
ckfijkvkfgimbkfvnfgkh,fgbl vbkdfb,
dfmbkjdfghfklhdf,bv;cbfdb b..b'b.,fb
,.fhkltyhkrthl;,

hello,
can we meet to
discuss the project

ciphered text

sender encrypts the
message using the
public key

receiver decrypts
the received messages
using his/her perivate
key

Fig 8.2: Public key encryption stages

(Rivest-Shamir-Adelman) which can be used both for encryption and for signing. It is generally considered to be secure when sufficiently long keys are used (up to 1024 or 2048 bits). RSA is currently the most important public-key algorithm, and is patented in the United States (expires year 2000), and free elsewhere.

Another major advantage of public-key systems is authentication, a basic requirement for telelearning settings. The fact that a user can sign a message digitally is critical in assuring that the message is from who claims to be the sender and that only the intended receiver can read it, while keeping the information about his private key safe and secret. Authentication under symmetric-key systems, on the other hand, requires the sharing of some secret information, which can violate the security objectives.

One disadvantage of using public-key cryptography for encryption is speed. Several symmetric-key encryption methods are significantly faster than any currently available public-key encryption mechanism. In order to get the best of both methods, public-key cryptography can be combined with symmetric key cryptography. For instance, the public key system can be used to encrypt a secret key used to encrypt the message. When receiving the message, the user first, decrypts the secret key using his private key, then uses the secret key to decrypt the message itself. This combines the high speed advantage of the symmetric system with the key-management convenience of public-key cryptography.

Another main issue with public-key crypto-systems is key management. Typically, it is the key owners responsibility to create their public and private keys. Since it is the user that generates the key pair, one of the problems is how can a recipient be sure that the public key claimed to be from the intended recipient is not that of an enemy pretending to be the recipient. All public key cryptographic protocols use what security experts call the idea of "Web of Trust". Anyone generating a public key is advised to have it signed by a Certification Authority, CA, which is in effect affirming that the key belongs to the person it claims to belong to. Web based public key repositories are provided by some security organizations or by an international key retrieval systems, such as Four 11 which offers a offers a White Pages e-mail directory including certified PGP (Pretty Good Privacy) keys.

An example of a commercial CA is Verisign Inc., a branch of RSA data Security Inc. The issued certificate tells the receiver that the certifying authority vouches for the fact that the public key really belongs to the sender identified on the certificate. This allows users to use public keys with confidence, as long as the certifying authority is trustworthy.

Certificates issued by CAs can be very advantageous for Internet-based telelearning settings, primarily for official or legal document exchanges between the virtual institution and telelearners. Also, students might need such a secure service when acquiring non-published, or any other form of important data from business or government organizations, for term projects and papers.

To sign a certificate, the Certification Authority demands documentation demonstrating the relation of the user of the key to the claimed person using the key. This has the advantage of establishing trust and reliability of message exchanges, but its drawback is that the cost may be high depending on the extent to which the CA checks the credentials of the key holder. Examples range from certificate pumps, which issue certificates without checking any credentials, to CA's that require the individual to present themselves in person with photo identification. CAs that require fingerprinting and retinal scans are unlikely to be required for telelearning purposes. For extra security purposes, digital certificates are only valid for a limited time. This means that certifying digital certificates commercially is a periodic and increasing cost. For an Internet-based telelearning setting, it is the virtual institution which would need a commercial service for their digital keys certification, especially if it was willing to deliver legal and sensitive documents on-line such as electronic degrees. Students, on the other hand, are very likely to use the cheaper and simpler encryption methods.

Secure Hash Functions

A secure hash function is another cryptographic method, which complements the two previously discussed cryptographic systems by fulfilling the remaining security elements: integrity and accountability. The main role of a cryptographic hash function is to provide digital signatures. This function is of great value to telelearners as it permits private messages, such as in the case of exams and teacher-student feedback, to be exchanged, while assuring the receiver (telelearner or instructor) about the identity of the sender.

Digital signatures are used to check for any forgery or tampering, and to assert the identity of the sender. To add a digital signature, the security program generates a mathematical "summary" of the message, called a hash or a digest, encrypts the hash with the sender's private key, and transmits the sender's public key along with the message. On the other end, the recipient verifies the signature by decrypting the hash using the sender's public key. If the hash is still a true summary of the message, then the message has arrived intact. If verification fails, that implies that the message might have been altered while being transmitted, or the signature is falsified. It is sometimes difficult, however to determine whether there was an attempted fraudulence or simply a transmission error.

One of the commonly used message digest algorithms is MD (Message Digest), and its versions: MD2, MD4 and MD5. MD5 is he most commonly used version. MD* algorithms are used for digital signature applications where a large message is hashed before being signed with the private key. All three algorithms generate a 128-bit digest from any length of input message.

The SSL Protocol

The SSL protocol provides server authentication, data encryption, and message integrity. SSL is layered beneath application protocols, such as HTTP, Telnet, FTP, Gopher and NNTP and above the connection protocol TCP/IP. The benefit of such structure is that it allows SSL to operate independently of the Internet application protocols. Moreover, by implementing SSL on both the client and the server site, the data is transmitted in encrypted form to ensure privacy.

A user can tell whether a document comes from a secure server by looking at the door key at the bottom of the Netscape window. The icon consists of a door-key, padlock or similar icon to show secure documents and a broken key or open padlock to show insecure documents.

The version of SSL that is exportable from the US is restricted to 40 bit keys. This implies that it is very likely to be broken by anyone with access to a reasonable amount of computing power, such as students in a computer department. In a report issued in January 1996, Whitfield Diffie, the inventor of public key cryptography, stated that a minimum of 75 bits was necessary for "adequate protection against the most serious threats". An improved, more secure implementation of SSL, called SSLeay, which was developed in Australia and is freely available and is being used by several WWW servers.

In general, SSL is among the most supported security protocols despite some of its limitations. The availability of more flexible protocols, such as SHTTP will be examined in the following paragraph. This popularity can be contributed primarily to the strong position of Netscape in the market place.

The S-HTTP Protocol

S-HTTP is a secure variant of http developed by Enterprise Integration Technologies (EIT). S-HTTP uses a modified version of HTTP clients and server to general purpose session and transaction security services, which include confidentiality, authentication, message integrity and non-repudiation of origin. It supports end-to-end security by incorporating cryptography to messages at the application level. This is contrary to the HTTP authorization mechanisms which require the client to attempt access and be denied before the security system is applied. S-HTTP incorporates public key cryptography from RSA Data Security in addition to supporting traditional shared-secret (password).

S-HTTP cryptographic features used are: the symmetric-key encryption for encrypting data, public-key encryption to ensure privacy and authentication of the transmitted data, and the hashing functions for ensuring integrity and authentication. Depending on the user' security needs, any combination of these three options can be used.

S-HTTP users deem S-HTTP to be more flexible than SSL in many cases. One main advantage of S-HTTP over SSL is its ability to perform client authentication. This allows for secure client/server sessions to be established. The fact that it requires the use of a certified public key, however, limits the degree to which it may be applied.

It is important to note that many of the new WWW developments can bring in new vulnerabilities to this medium. For instance, the Java, the VRML, and the multimedia web conferencing operations involve heavy use of graphics, audio and video. These applications can encumber the existing encryption systems and can lead to attempts to circumvent security features in order to maintain real time throughput, such as during a real time on-line class lecture. Generally, since any new technology or feature is likely to be vulnerable to security attacks when it is first introduced, early adopters should always watch for such risks.

Security at the IP Network Layer

Within a telelearning environment, virtual on-line educational institutions are usually open to public access for students and guest visitors to consult the available courses and services. The more traffic and the more services are running through the server, the higher is the risk of ending up with security problems.

One common security control tool is the network firewall. Firewalls provide security at the network level by acting as a guard against any untrusted traffic, and by monitoring and controlling the flow of information between the Internet and the institution's network.

An Internet firewall is a system or a hybrid of systems that enforces access control policy between a private network and the Internet. It usually combines a pair of mechanisms: one to block traffic and another to permit it.

Generally, firewalls are configured to support authentication mechanisms in order to ensure that only authorized users can log into the protected resources, which is very important in hampering intruders from accessing any unauthorized material. More sophisticated firewalls block traffic from the outside to the inside, but permit users on the inside to communicate freely with the outside. Some even act as very effective auditing tools. Their main functions are: to maintain internal information about the state of connections passing through them and the contents of some of the data streams, and to provide summaries to the administrator about what kinds and amount of traffic passed through it and how many attempts there were to break into it.

The main elements of a firewall are:

- *The screening or filtering router:* a screening router is a basic component of most firewalls. It can be a commercial router or a host-based router with some kind of packet filtering capability. Screening routers, typically are able to block traffic between the private network and the Internet, and disable any TCP/IP direct forwarding to the private network. Some firewalls, simply consist of a screening host between the two networks.
- *The bastion host:* the bastion is the most critical element of the firewall. It is usually on the private network and is the only reachable point by the Internet.

There are several firewall configurations, which can be applied to secure private networks. The most secure configuration is the screened host gateway. In addition to the high security level it provides, screened host gateway is easy to implement. A bastion host is configured on the private network, with a screening router between the Internet and the private network, which only permits Internet access to the bastion host. Since the bastion host is on the private network, problems with external routing configurations are obstructed. The zone of risk in a screened gateway is restricted to the bastion host, and the screening router. Figure 8.3 portrays the screening host gateway

Despite their useful characteristics, firewalls still have several shortcomings, which need to be worked on. Even though firewalls are increasingly deployed and constantly proliferating, no new consequential developments in other aspects of security have been added. Analysts believe that, to be effective, a firewall must be integrated with other technologies such as digital certificates and cryptography methods. Other problem areas include the following:

• A firewall can't protect the network from internal users and attacks that don't go through the firewall. Inside threats can be as damaging to the network as external attackers. Inside users can steal, damage and copy data, actions that a firewall can't detect. A firewall must be a part of a consistent overall organizational security architecture. User education and internal security measures are very important in this case in order to limit similar problems.

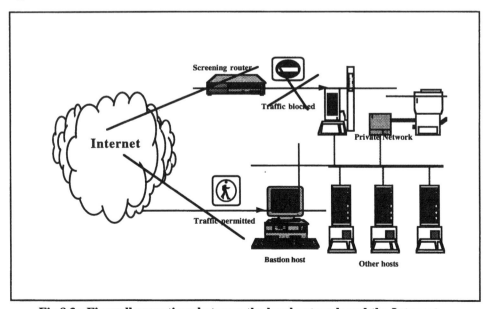

Fig 8.3 : Firewall operations between the local network and the Internet

• A firewall can't protect against viruses. Although firewalls can control the incoming traffic, the scanning is mostly for source and destination addresses, not for the details of the data. Even though filtering methods are becoming more sophisticated, the various ways of encoding binary files for transfer over networks, the numerous architectures and too many viruses, and the use of different ways to hide data, significantly lower the efficiency of the firewall.

The increasing number of new types of viruses, and methods a virus can use to hide data, significantly lower the efficiency of firewalls.

The level of expertise required to install and maintain a firewall, depend on the services provided, the platform used, and the institution's security concerns. Most of the firewalls available these days are very practical as they require basic Internet skills to obtain the tools and basic administration skills to configure, compile and install them. A dedicated staff or staff member might be required for the continuous maintenance of the tool, in which case an extra cost will be incurred by the institution.

E-mail Security

E-mail is an important component of telelearning traffic. E-mail sent over the Internet is more like paper mail on a postcard than mail in a sealed envelope. It can easily be read, or even altered, by hackers who can read and/or forge the transmitted messages. Its high popularity and easy use makes it vulnerable to such attacks. Securing e-mail, therefore, is a very critical requirement for safe message transmissions.

Several protocols and encryption systems have been developed in order to fulfill the enhanced security requirement. These include mainly: PGP, PEM and MOSS. Many of these systems were also used for other Internet applications such as file encryption.

All of the e-mail encryption systems available today, provide the following common features, which are fundamental for a telelearning environment . These include:

Sender authentication: which ensures the instructor that the received message (which can be a paper, a test, etc.) is truly from the student who claims to have sent it. Sender authentication is provided by digital signature. Validation of the sender is also

	important for students, especially when receiving important class material form their instructor, or personal feedback.
Message integrity:	ensures that the message has not been altered in an unauthorized manner. This is also critical for similar situations as in the case of authentication.
Non-repudiation of origin:	where the originator (either the telelearner or the instructor) can not deny having sent the message.
Message confidentiality:	which ensures that the message is protected against tampering or disclosure to unauthorized individuals. This is realized by encrypting the message using symmetric or asymmetric (public key) cryptography algorithms. This feature is very important for telelearning practitioners, mainly for on-line submission of tests and papers, which must be protected form any cheating or tampering attempts.

Despite their security capabilities, each of these protocols still has some inadequacy which limit their efficiency.

PGP: Pretty Good Privacy

PGP is the first protocol which was developed to provide E-mail security, and is the most commonly used standard program for secure e-mail and file encryption. It is a public key system, which uses the RSA public key cipher as follows. First, it encrypts the message using a secret key. Then, it encrypts the key using the recipient's public key. When the recipient receives the message, PGP uses the recipient's private key to decrypt the secret key and then uses that decrypted key to decipher the message.

PGP can be also used to sign messages, which helps authenticating and verifying their integrity. It does so by first computing a "hash" of the message using a hash function such as MD5 or SHA. It then, encrypts the hash output (e.g. 128 bits or 16 bytes) with the sender's secret key. In order to validate the message's origin, the recipient uses the sender's public key to decrypt the signature, and calculates the same hash output of the received message. If the output to this decryption agrees with the recipients calculated hash output, then the recipient is knows that the sender actually sent that message, and that the message has not been changed.

In addition to satisfying the different security objectives, PGP also helps users to manage their keys by allowing them to create their own private and public keys. Like any other public key users, PGP users also face the users' trust issue discussed under public-key cryptography . One reliable resource for PGP public key users is the FOUR 11 site, which includes a comprehensive list of the public keys it certified.

PEM: Privacy Enhanced Mail

PEM (Privacy Enhanced Mail) is another system for encrypting mail and making digital signatures. It has been made a standard, but is not as widely used as PGP. PEM has several implementations available such as: rpem and ripem.

Like PGP, PEM catches the main essential security services: encryption, authentication, integrity and certificate-based key management but it does not provide authentication of the recipient. Being a practical standard, PEM can be used with almost every existing e-mail system and someone else who is using PEM.

In PGP, the signature of a message cannot be verified while the message is encrypted. This means that third-parties cannot verify the originator of a message. PEM users cannot send unsigned messages at all, but this is possible with MOSS, the new version of PEM, which will be described in the following paragraph.

MOSS: MIME Object Security Services

MOSS is a specification that integrates the security services of PEM with MIME. MOSS replaces PEM, and has many advantages:

• It does not require certificates.
• It allows e-mail addresses and arbitrary strings for identifying the public keys of users, instead of only distinguished names.
• It allows non-text messages including images, voice, video, and structured combinations of contents.

Unfortunately, MOSS is not interoperable with PGP, and it does not provide symmetric encryption services.

Secure/Multipurpose Internet Mail Extensions

S/MIME is another e-mail security protocol which adds security to e-mail messages in MIME format. S/MIME provides authentication (using digital signatures) and privacy (using a symmetric cipher, and a public-key algorithm). The most important feature of S/MIME is its interoperability, which assures that any two packages that implement S/MIME can communicate securely. S/MIME is not a standard yet, but is in the process of standardization. Compared to the three previously described protocols (PGP, PEM and MOSS), is more flexible, more scaleable and provides a better interoperability, which explains its widening acceptance among Internet users.

Voice Security

Voice is becoming a more common application over the Internet. Within a telelearning environment, when a real time lecture or discussion held using a text based interactive tool such as MOO, MUD or IRC is supported with voice can significantly enhance communication effectiveness. In many cases, vocal conversations need to be encrypted, such as in the case of oral tests, or private group discussions. In order to fulfill the need of privacy, several voice security applications have been developed which use different cryptographic protocols and compression techniques. Some of these tools include: Speak Freely for Windows and Netfone its counterpart for UNIX (Sun, SGI). Both permit encrypted conversations over Internet or modem connections. Another commonly used security application is PGPFone (Pretty Good Privacy Phone), which, as its name indicates, uses the PGP protocol.

MBONE Security

Like any other technology operating over the Internet, security over the MBONE is very crucial, both for the applications and for the networks receiving the multicast packets. Because of the open architecture of the Internet, the MBONE, at its current state, is very vulnerable to external attacks and intruders attempting to spy on and listen to the multicasted sessions.

For an Internet-based telelearning setting using the MBONE, security is considered as a very central requirement, which should be vouched for, especially when holding professional training classes and private lectures, where access should be limited to the registered students. Other cases where security has to be warranted are during on-line presentations, where the transmitted material has to be delivered without any alterations, such as the case of medical images being exchanged between multiple sites.

Applications Security

Most MBONE applications today, such as SDR, WB and VAT, embody some security features such as encryption.

A case in point is SDR, the session directory tool of the MBONE, which permits for private announcements and advertising of sessions and provides the option of holding both private and public sessions. Secret sessions, though, should use the same announcement mechanism as public sessions in order to ensure that their bandwidth is taken into account, and that their multicast addresses are not inadvertently re-used. To do so, SDR advertises the secure sessions twice: once unencrypted with little information about its bandwidth, contact information and multicast addresses, and once encrypted with all of the information including encryption keys for the media tools.

To create a private session, SDR must be pre-configured with a set of private group names and their encryption keys. For increased security, these keys could be exchanged using encryption mechanisms such as PEM (Privacy Enhanced Mail), or through a fax or a telephone. The encryption keys for these groups are not displayed on the interface at any time, and they are themselves stored encrypted in a file. When a private session is selected, a user can only take part in that session if he/she enters a password to SDR to allow the decryption of the key file of the group. As the MBONE technology becomes more mature, security techniques will gradually become more sophisticated and efficient, promising a safe and secure real time multimedia environment.

Network Security

Security over networks using the MBONE is a fundamental requirement for securing the networks from risks, such as receiving malicious packets hiding a Trojan horse or any other type of virus, which can be very damaging for the entire network.

The most common way used to protect the traditional networks is using firewalls. In a like manner, networks running with the MBONE technology also uses firewalls to secure its operations. As described earlier under the section, " Security at the IP layer," the Internet routers are configured to filter out any unwanted traffic or harmful packets, and hence called filters and form a firewall between the local network and the rest of the global Internet. The distinct feature of MBONE filters is that they are configured to allow only IP multicast packets and IGMP message query and update packets to flow into and out of the network. As was mentioned in chapter 2, "MBONE protocols" it is only those hosts who expressed interest in joining the session by sending IGMP query messages, and subscribed to the group multicast address, who can send and receive data . It is the filter's duty, therefore to inspect the incoming UDP data stream for unwanted UDP packets or non-UDP protocols.

Chapter 9

■

Policy Issues

At the moment, the Internet-based telelearning paradigm is still at its early stages, and has not yet established itself as one of the universally accepted and well recognized academic settings. This chapter identifies several policy issues which are still encumbering certain learning and teaching activities, and might be representing major impediments to telelearners, and suggests ways in which they could be solved.

In this chapter, we will investigate four principal policy issues which are of major importance to telelearners and instructors via the Internet. These are: copyright, accreditation of on-line degrees, on-line academic fraud and evaluation of Web sites' content and author.

Although a comprehensive discussion of these issues, especially legal aspects of copyright is beyond the scope of this book, we will be highlighting some of the problem areas, and will provide an overall review of each issue.

Copyright Issue

The Internet's wide-open nature and universality, combined with technologies which allow the easy digitization of any type of information, are creating several copyright problems for both copyright holders as well as the Internet users.

New technologies allowing for easy digitization of different types of intellectual material such as text, graphics, audio and video, software, and photographs, bring with them opportunities to use copyrighted material illegally, such as making free unlicensed copies, modifying them, and distributing them.

Within an Internet-based telelearning environment, easy on-line accessibility to intellectual information, whether copyrighted or not, is fundamental for an effective on-line dissemination of educational material. The unsolved copyright issues of on-line intellectual material can, in many cases, impede on-line students and instructors from benefiting from the Web's resources to their full potential. In many other cases, telelearning practitioners might even find themselves involved in unlawful acts of copyright infringements without even knowing or intending it.

Some stakeholders believe that even browsing the Internet constitutes a reproduction and can result in copyright infringement. According to their argument, a distinction between downloading and accessing a document is not possible. In order to browse a document, it must be first accessed and then downloaded. Once displayed on the screen, the document can be easily copied to the hard drive, which is a reproduction.

Furthermore, the international aspect of the Internet makes it easy for any Internet user with a powerful PC to illegally reproduce copyrighted documents, without risking, in most of the cases, being tracked or legally sued.

One other problem that aggravates the copyright issue for copyright holders is the strongly established Internet culture and belief that Internet material is free, and that it should be widely disseminated.

When it comes to using the Internet material for telelearning, users can be easily entrapped into copyright infringement, unintentionally, in most of the cases. This is mainly because of the unclear rules and the lack of user education about when and what acts constitute a copyright infringement.

Based on a DEOS-L (Distance Education On-Line Symposium) discussion about how to overcome the copyright of electronic material handicaps, several members supported the suggestion that on-line instructors should be looking primarily to the different government sites, since they cannot be copyrighted. However, in many cases, the subject related data and information is inadequate, or is non-existent, in such sites.

In case copyrighted on-line material is required, participants believed that it is always better to have the copyright owner's permission than not to ask and be in trouble later on. Based on the experience of some of the discussion participants, many owners of copyrighted digital material, mainly other educational institutions, government agencies and several corporations, were very cooperative and willing to allow them to use their Web sites for educational purposes.

The following are some cases of illegitimate acts, which can take place while operating within a telelearning environment:

One of the very common situations is when students need to write a multimedia document and present it in class. In order to supplement their work with the necessary material, students might need to integrate several forms of multimedia files, such as photographs, audio and video clips, which are in most of the cases, other people's creation and are copyrighted. Using them without permission is a clear violation of the owner's copyright rights.

Another case, where many telelearning practitioners are unlikely to consider it to be a violation, is when instructors use some Web sites to complement their lectures by copying the sites contents into Powerpoint slides. As one member of the DEOS-L mailing list puts it, copying (the Web page content) into a Powerpoint presentation constitutes a copy, and therefore a copyright infringement.

The same effect occurs when telelearning practitioners, whether instructors, students or even administration staff, build up Web pages with several links to other people's copyrighted material on the Web. The WWW is considered to be an electronic form of publication. Therefore, if anyone intends to publish Web pages containing any material from someone else's Web site, he/she must have the permission of the authors of the original work to avoid liability under copyright law. This applies not only to whole works, but also to sections of works, such as passages of texts, pictures, etc.

The main point worth noting about the previous examples is that the Web pages include material which is not only created by the Web page owner, but also by others. The copyrights of the embodied links in many cases have not been obtained. Therefore, using that material for presentations or for integration in other works can be a copyright infringement, which goes beyond the page creator, and involves others who have a vested interest in using the page material.

Another case of infringements that are likely to occur unwittingly within a telelearning environment is posting other people's material on the net without the person's permission. A case in point is when instructors post any type of material (articles, sections from books, photographs, audio and video clips) thinking that this act falls under fair dealing, where using other people's work for educational and research purposes doesn't constitute a copyright infringement.

In view of the difficulties these situations pose for a telelearning environment, quick solutions to these issues are essential.

One easy and rapid alternative is to contact the original author for permission. This can be either by writing to the Webmaster of the site, or by looking up the person's name in one of the Web electronic directories. However, it is not always easy to reach the Web site's creator. For this reason, a clear policy needs to be outlined in order to make legal reproduction of educational material easier, clear and less complex.

Copyright laws all over the world, as well as international copyright agreements blur when it comes to the Internet. Similar to the governments attempts to solve this issue, the Canadian government, in 1994, has created the Information Highway Advisory Council (IHAC), in attempt to develop a national strategy to allow it to cope with the challenges of the information technology environment. One of the important responsibilities of the council was to review the Canadian copyright law in the context of the new information technologies, such as the Internet, and to come up with recommendations relating to copyrights of on-line multimedia works, browsing and fair dealing. This duty was delegated to a Copyright Subcommittee which involved two main stakeholders:

• *Copyright owners:* such as agencies representing musicians, authors, newspaper producers, radio and television directors, and photographer, who were concerned about legal protection of their properties.
• *User groups:* which comprised educational institutions, researchers, libraries, and Internet users, who believe that since the Internet is presumed to provide universal access to intellectual material, there should be no barriers to reach on-line material and that the government should limit the copyright protection.

The Copyright Subcommittee's report later served as a basis for the council's final report and included several recommendations. The following paragraphs highlight the principal recommendations of the IHAC subcommittee, which relate to digital intellectual property copyright.

Principles

The government should set clear principles to help address the digital material copyrights issue, which would help the learning community, which is a major user of these works, in understanding the amended legislation. These principles should be principally based on:

• Balancing the creators rights and the requirements of the users (including the education and learning environment) to have an easy access to those works.
• Providing the users community with the necessary help to understand the need for the legislation, and developing programs to explain how the law

should be implemented. Users should understand that copyright protection is crucial to ensuring that creators, producers and distributors are rewarded for their effort and investment. Such compensation will encourage copyright owners to give more contributions to the learning and educational environment.

Multimedia Works

Even though some stakeholders suggested a more specific definition of digital multimedia works, the council believed that the category Compilation adequately defines multimedia works. Further, they were convinced that digital works do not represent a new category of works, but it's rather a different way of presenting works. Therefore no amendments should be made under this section.

Including a technology specific definition of digital work, like what some stakeholders, such as the Canadian Association of Photographers, suggested, would require frequent amendments to the law. The fast technological developments and the time required to introduce statutory regulations will result in outdated definitions.

Browsing

As discussed earlier, browsing copyrighted digitized material is a confusing element. In its final report, the council recommended that the Copyright Act should be amended to clarify what constitutes browsing and infringements by browsing, and what works are publicly available; include a definition of browse. The Council agreed with the copyright subcommittee in that the act of browsing a work in a digital environment (which includes the Internet) should be considered an act of reproduction. Their suggested definition was: Browse means a temporary materialization of a work on a video screen, television monitor or similar device, or the performance of the portion of such work on a speaker or similar device by a user, but does not include the making of a permanent reproduction of the work in a material form.

Council members representing copyright holders considered that browsing could mean either accessing the work, or making a copy. User groups on the other hand, felt that this would limit access to these works, since even simple access with purpose of determining whether the file would be needed or not, can result in an infringement. The final recommendation was that creator should be able to identify when and what parts of their works can be browsed and be publicly available.

Fair Dealing

During the Copyright Subcommittee discussions, user groups, principally educational institutions, were arguing that since it is very important for the Internet material to be widely disseminated to promote universal education, free access to on-line information and its availability for the open public should fall under section 27(2) of the Canadian copyright act. It states: The following acts do not constitute an infringement of copyright: any fair dealing with any work for the purposes of private study, research, criticism, review or newspaper summary.

In its final report, the council was of the opinion that the fair dealing provisions don't need to be amended, and that they apply to the digital material. These provisions however, should be made more clear and more specific, to help user groups understand the scope of the fair dealing exceptions and the nature of copyright liability.

Moral Rights

Under the Copyright act, moral rights are defined to protect both the integrity of the work and the author's reputation. According to section 14.1 of the Copyright act, infringement takes place when the work is *distorted, mutilated, or otherwise modified or used in association with a product, service, cause or institution* resulting in biasing the author's reputation. Infringement of these rights is very easy over the Internet using the free available software, which can filter messages and modify document contents, by changing colors, removing parts etc.

User groups were convinced that certain information, such as government statistics, regulations and laws should be made widely available. It is in the public's interest therefore and very important to protect the integrity of this type of data by preventing users from modifying them. The council recommended that the government should make government information available without requiring any payments or authorization, a very helpful requirement for the learning community. Further, the council advised that the legal framework governing copyrights should ensure, rather than curtail, the development of systems to monitor the uses of copyrights of on-line digital material.

Administration

In order to ensure an effective administration of the copyright law, the council recommended a combination of technological, policy and legislative solutions to be used.

Some of the technological solutions include:

- *Encryption:* as discussed under Chapter 8: "Security Issues", encryption is one of the effective solutions to ensure security. Applying this technology to a multipoint system, however, becomes more complex and could involve high administrative costs.
- *Electronic fingerprinting*: this technology involves taking a virtual electronic fingerprinting of the CPU or the system, and uses it as a key to encrypt personal secret keys, IDs and passwords onto the user's hard drive. The system's token is never stored in clear text anywhere, and if illegally moved from the original computer system, it will not operate and becomes useless, as each system has its own unique electronic fingerprint. In order to move the application, the fingerprint must be uninstalled then moved. This keeps applications from illegally multiplying at a customer's site.
- *Tagging*: is a method used for inserting a copyright notice or other message into the protected work to inform users that no illegal copies should be made. Tags can be the name and registration number inserted into a software program, or a logo of an organization. For copyright, the Copyright Subcommittee suggested inserting a copyright notice scattered throughout the content.
- *Conversion/Anti-Copying:* This technology involves transforming the digital work into an intermediary form so that the original information cannot be edited or altered. By applying this method, unauthorized reproduction is impeded since the quality of the work diminishes with each successive copy.
- *Copy prohibition:* copy prohibition can be realized by including bits in the digital content which preclude copying on certain electronic machines. When the file is downloaded or is being read by the machine, the saving (or recording) function is disabled.
- *Digital coding:* One of the examples that the Copyright Subcommittee included to illustrate the efficiency of this method in securing digitized materials, is the digital coding technique developed by CyberTech Systems Inc. The main characteristics of that code is that it is inaudible, unremovable, automatically copied and can be used on anything that utilizes a soundtrack.

By replicating only a portion of the digital numbers and randomly scattering the remaining invisible numbers in the audio tracks, no modification of the soundtrack is possible without removing a part of the soundtrack. Moreover, the manipulation of the code creates residue codes to prevent tampering. As a result, any attempts of tampering the audio track are hampered.

With respect to policy measures, the council was convinced that the government should support and assist the industry in the development and use of the technological solutions. This can be, for instance, by standardizing the technologies and educating users and creators about their use. Further, IHAC advised that the government should take an active role, in partnership with industry and the creator and user communities, in a public education campaign to better inform users and creators about the use of the copyright.

Regarding legislative actions, it was suggested to include a section under the amended copyright act, stating that any manipulation or attempts to break the copyguards or encryption technologies with the purpose of transgressing the work's copyright is considered a criminal offense.

Public Education

Informing users and owners of copyrighted digitized intellectual material about the rights and responsibilities of each party is very critical to ensure that the act is effectively and flawlessly implemented. The council concluded that public education is a shared responsibility between the government and the user and creators group. In their opinion, users as well as creators, have the duty to educate themselves about the digital material copyright.

When it comes to Internet users, including the telelearning community, the Copyright Subcommittee believed that changing the wide perception, or netiquette, that the Internet is a free zone for the open and unrestricted exchange of information, whether it is proprietary or not, should be changed through an extensive education campaign. First, the program should use extensive advertising, which can create a new impression that infringing digital materials copyright is a criminal offense. Next, academic institutions should be involved to ensure that their students and faculty have a clear understanding of the copyright principles. With more on-line educational institutions using the Internet resources as their principal source of information, an important section in the course curriculum should be included to teach students about their duties and rights when using copyright digital material and what constitutes an infringement.

The council members further suggested that the government takes an active role, during these campaigns by leading as an example in implementing the new regulations, and participating in enforcement programs.

Following these recommendations, Industry Canada has started working on the different sections of the proposal by designating focus groups to discuss the different Internet liability issues, chiefly the issue of who should be liable over the Internet.

The open anarchy and the international aspect of the Internet means that Copyright law amendments should not be restricted to the national level. Given the importance of the Internet, the threat of copyright infringement is an issue affecting all countries. Even if instructors or students, or any other Internet users, are deprived from downloading a national copyright holder's material (textbooks, photographs, audio and video), they can still violate the rights of a foreign copyright holder, without the risk of being tracked or punished.

Even though, today, there is no common international copyright law, international copyright agreements exist, like the Berne Convention and the Universal Copyright Convention, which are the primary sources of international copyright law. These conventions might provide some basic help, but they still need to be expanded upon. By harmonizing the different legislation and improving the international treaties, mainly by adding clear and specific definitions of what constitutes a violation of an Internet copyrighted document, unauthorized material could be better protected.

Accreditation

Judging the quality of the delivered academic programs and degrees is a very important issue for many stakeholders including: telelearners and their families, academic institutions, sponsoring bodies, governments, and employers, especially when the program is offered at an international level. Already hundreds of courses and degrees are being offered on-line today, and competition is starting to intensify.

The low costs involved in developing and publishing an on-line course and creating virtual educational institutions, along with the students' need for more flexible educational services, have significantly encouraged this shift in the educational environment. One of the main implications of this change is that telelearners are very likely to have difficulties deciding about the program to follow and the courses to choose, while ensuring that they made the right choice.

One other issue is that educational standards and evaluation criteria of degrees and programs can vary widely from one country to another, and sometimes even within the same country. Moreover, dealing with students scattered all over the world, who will later use their on-line degrees in diversified and dissimilar job markets, represents big challenge for virtual educational institutions, since the degree has to satisfy the telelearners local job market requirements.

When selecting an on-line course or program, students need to be sure that their learning experience and the earned degree is equal in value, or even better than if the same course was taken with a conventional institution. Furthermore, they have to be convinced that their degree will be accepted by other existing educational systems, and that credits transfer to or from other programs (on-line or traditional) is feasible. These requirements are of big importance for telelearners, especially those who strive to build their career using the received degree, in contrast to other on-line students who might be taking courses just to improve their aptitudes or to increase their knowledge in some areas.

One of the fundamental objectives of on-line institutions is to guarantee the universal access of the public to educational resources and high quality learning material. Lacking the means to assure the telelearning community about the quality of their programs, can limit the on-line institution's target market to local levels and lower their enrollment rate, which contradicts their primary objective of universal reach.

Another side effect of the lack of accreditation standards is that students can be discouraged and confused when evaluating whether the program is really worth its costs or not. To cite an instance, basing one's choice on criteria such as tuition fees can be, in many cases, misleading. Even though some subscription fees are high, they might not reflect a high quality program. Also wrong assumptions about the appropriate time needed to finish the course might incorrectly reflect the effectiveness of the program and can result in costly wrong decisions.

Issues like these, and others, urge the need for the development of accreditation bodies for assessing and evaluating on-line programs. Accreditation is a rigorous evaluation process that is guided by a defined set of evaluation criteria established by the accreditation body. This includes numerous stages of team evaluation and on-site peer review and evaluation visits. Accreditation plays an important role in every student's professional life. Graduates from nonaccredited institutions would have less job and advancement opportunities than their peers from accredited institutions or programs. For the job market, accreditation offers industry a certain minimum guarantee of the skills they can expect in job applicants, and therefore it promotes high quality work environments. As quoted in a California School of Independent Schools accreditation article, "....accreditation is a means for fostering excellence in education and encouraging improvement through self-study and evaluation." It also enables the institution to develop a clear set of goals and objectives and promotes continuous controls and reviews for its strategies to ensure that all objectives are satisfied.

Similar to the accreditation process followed when evaluating traditional courses and degrees, national accreditation organizations should be involved in applying standards for assessing on-line programs. Today, a number of professional associations have established accreditation councils for specific programs and courses offered in conventional universities. Extending these organization's activities to on-line programs would promote on-line accreditation processes. One point worth noting, though, is that these councils may have to amend or add new criteria to their accreditation parameters used for conventional programs. Two of the new measures are:

• Evaluating if the new telelearning setting affects the telelearners learning and the efficiency of the programs activities.
• Assessing the support level provided on-line by the faculty with regards to all the students needs.

Since the most powerful aspect of virtual institutions is their international reach, recognition of these programs across the international borders is an exigency across. At this time, there are two global accrediting agencies: The International Accreditation Commission for Post Secondary Educational Institutions and the World Association of Universities and Colleges. Accreditation by these agencies is based on a thorough evaluation of the academic programs of the institution, the institution's instructional resources, its financial stability and its professional integrity.

These already existing bodies can extend their activities to involve the on-line programs, which promotes establishing confidence in the offered on-line programs, and helps validate the integrity and the quality of the on-line Internet-based programs. One evaluation element however, which might be considered less important for virtual institutions than for the conventional ones is the value and the availability of the instructional resources. Since all institutions will be using the same source of instructional material: the Internet. Therefore, all telelearners will be using ubiquitous resources of equal value to everybody.

Further, reciprocal accreditation recognition could be established between other already existing national accreditation agencies which accredit programs within single disciplines in order to promote the international acceptance of on-line degrees. These procedures are likely to be uncomplicated and smooth, especially for disciplines with a universal aspect like the scientific and engineering field. A case in point, is *The Accreditation Board for Engineering and Technology (ABET), Inc.* which has begun development of reciprocal accreditation recognition on mutual recognition of evaluation programs implemented in Australia, Canada, Ireland, New Zealand, United Kingdom, Hong Kong, and the United States. As a result, professionals from any of these countries could practice without any restriction from other country members.

Like the conventional programs' accreditation procedures, accreditation of on-line programs can involve the same procedures, which include:

• First, using the set of criteria of the national accreditation body or the international council, the on-line institution faculty conduct a self assessment of the quality of their program.
• Next, members from already accredited on-line institutions, selected by the national accreditation body or the international committee, evaluate the program by examining its different elements and interviewing students and staff members, then write an evaluation report to be submitted to the international committee.
• Finally, based on its set of criteria, which focus mainly on issues related to program quality, integrity and student support, a committee from the international accrediting council (which also constitutes a number of faculty staff and experienced educators in Internet-based telelearning) reviews the assessment report and recommendations, then makes a judgment and publishes it on-line for the general public.

By publicly announcing the decision, the committee proves the accountability of the institution and assures the telelearning community about the program's quality.

As with traditional programs, it can be anticipated that many high quality on-line institutions might balk at the accreditation process and refuse to consider submitting to it, if it is like the present accreditation processes: expensive, lengthy, and complex. Therefore, universities today often follow program guidelines from a professional agency, such as the Data Processing

Management Association (DPMA), and the Association for Computer Machinery (ACM), without that organization actually evaluating whether the guidelines are being followed.

Further, some requirements to earn accreditation might be difficult to satisfy. For instance, to be accredited a program needs students. However, since many students might not enroll in nonaccredited programs, the enrollment rate would be always low, depriving the institution from the various advantages which come with accreditation, such as the potential opportunities of increasing its enrollment rate and being among those seeking front positions in the Internet-based telelearning setting.

The idea of instituting an international accreditation body might be, in the short run, difficult and very time consuming to realize and to reach a compromise between the different accreditation criteria of worldwide national accreditation bodies. Its outcomes, however, are very significant for the telelearning community and in the long run it will play a major role in improving on-line education via the Internet.

It is likely that many on-line institutions and programs will be hybrids of contributions of multinational educators and staff. The main advantage of this diversity is that their contributions can help in setting a program, which will most likely satisfy many evaluation criteria elements of student with different cultures and backgrounds.

Academic Fraud

With the proliferation of on-line programs and virtual institutions, issues related to examination and evaluation, such as academic fraud and student credibility, are of major concern to many telelearning practitioners. Testing students is essential to determine how well students are meeting course objectives. They help to verify if the student assimilated the course material, and help in revealing any misunderstood, misapplied or poorly mastered material. These issues have been a hot topic on the Distance Education On-line Symposium (DEOS-L) mailing list.

Many on-line instructors believed that chances of academic fraud in on-line environments are higher than in traditional classes. When an on-line Internet medium is used for testing, such as text based conferencing tools, or WWW conferencing, preventing cheating is difficult since there is no way to force students to close books or to prevent them from getting help from somebody seated besides them. On the other hand, many other participants were convinced that academic fraud and plagiarism are not any riskier than in face-to-face classes. These concerns have been around for a long time, especially those of defining the student's identity, regardless of the class setting. One participant asked these questions in an attempt to justify this point:

• How can (on-line) instructors know that the student who took the on-line final exam is the same who took the course?
• How can they be assured that the student who hands in a paper in an on-campus, face-to-face course, or on-line, is the same student who researched and wrote the paper?

Both questions can be applied to any type of educational setting, whether on-line or face to face. Based on the participants' experiences, the incidences of fraud seemed to be low in face-to-face classes, and they are expecting that the same pattern would apply for on-line courses. It is true that by not having any imposed supervision some students might behave dishonestly. Some of the measures which can be applied in order to limit the risks of academic fraud is to apply a hybrid of technological and pedagogic solutions.

With regards to technology, several tools described in Chapter 8: "Security over the Internet" can help in limiting the risk of fraud. Such tools include: public and private encryption keys, passwords, system authentication and digital signatures.

Concerning the pedagogic methods, an instructor can apply the following measures:

• Including more group projects, case presentations and term papers in the curriculum. An instructor can either assign a heavier weight to these activities or use them as the only methods for evaluating students. This method is becoming more popular even in traditional face to face courses, and is proving to be an efficient method to help students assimilate better the course material by researching subjects deeply.
• Holding on-line text based or oral discussions, and basing evaluations on students' contributions during the discussions. The same media can be also used for on-line oral tests, where student are required to answer within a limited time.
• Setting exams in test centers under the supervision of assigned proctors, where the identity of students can be verified. This option might be very costly for the virtual institution, especially when students are widely

scattered within the same country or around the world.
- CyberHigh, an entirely on-line high school, tries to limit plagiarism and fraud by emphasizing in its academic policy that doing work for students is an immoral act, and that such acts deprive students from learning. As in-school teachers recognize their students' work, CyberHigh teachers use continuous interaction and work with the students as a means of helping them recognize their students' work.
- Once high-speed Internet access, and broad bandwidth over the Internet become widely available to the telelearning community, live audio and video presentations can provide big assistance in assessing the students' performance. For instance, students' presentations can significantly be enhanced as they will be integrating more multimedia files which can be of big assistance in conveying their ideas.

Despite the different solutions and measures used to restrict academic fraud, students operating within any milieu, be it on-line or not, and who are determined to act dishonestly, are likely to find ways to do so. As one DEOS-L participant put it: (instructors) keep raising the bar, and such students simply jump higher (or go under). Many others were of the view that since instructors trust their students when they see them, they should now learn to trust them just a little more when they don't. Moreover, since students trust their on-line instructors, likewise on-line instructors should trust their on-line students.

Applying a hybrid of the above suggested solutions can certainly raise a "reasonable bar" for the high-jumpers but this issue always remains to some extent the student's personal and moral responsibility more than an enforced discipline by the institution's authorities.

Evaluation of the Web Site's Content and Creator

Before any information over the Web is used, users, especially students researching material on their own, must be able to evaluate the site's content and its author's credentials in order to be assured about the accuracy, credibility and validity of the obtained information.

The low barriers for publishing over the Internet, and the prevailing netiquette of free-speech over the Net, requires Web users to be extremely critical consumers of information which comes through the World Wide Web. With the open nature of the Web which allows many unknown information providers, be it individuals, organizations, or associations, users, especially young telelearners, should be trained on adopting critical attitudes towards any material encountered on-line.

Before the Web, printed information resources, such as books, magazines, newspapers and even personal correspondence have been designed and written following a clear set of conventional guidelines, and structured formats, which agree with the expectations of the readers. A case in point, is that when reading a book, readers expect to find a biography about the author's background, previous works, as well as the educational level. In a newspaper article, a journalist is expected to present accurate information free of advertising.

With the emergence of the Web, traditional specifications no longer accord with Web documents. Web users today have to modify their criteria when judging the worth of on-line Web sites content. Most Web files come in nonlinear communication formats, with little or no information about their creators, their accountability, their motives and objectives behind building these sites.

Despite the dilemma a user can be trapped in while researching topics, setting a clear set of parameters against which the site's value can be assessed is essential for Web users, primarily telelearning environment members, to get the maximum benefits out of the invaluable Web resources. These criteria should emphasize elements such as: the authentication of the site's author, evaluation of credentials, assessing newness of the material, and evaluating the design and layout of the site.

The following section will describe some of the general guidelines for users, regardless of whether these are students or instructors, which could help them in evaluating Web sites' contents and their authorship.

Authenticate the Web Site Creator(s)

Determining who created the Web site, and from where the information originated is the foremost component to consider when evaluating a Web site's content. Even though many sites may not include direct information about their creator(s), many others either provide information in the title or somewhere in the front page, or in the form of hypertext links called About or Information or logos and question marks.

Unlike printed materials and books, which often include an editorial review or biography about writers, it is very rare that electronic files contain that type of information. In many cases, information about individuals is limited to an e-mail address, or to a link to the author's e-mail. When the developer is an organization, very often a brief introduction or description about its mission and objectives is available.

In case no link to any already existing on-line information about the author(s) is available, the e-mail address can help determining whether the author is an individual or a group, and the type of institution he/she or they are associated with. To illustrate, e-mail addresses with user name, Webmaster or Info often mean that a group of people are responsible of the site. For instance, education@info.apple.com, means that information about the institution can be provided by the person or group of people who are looking after that site.

When the user name in the e-mail address represents an individual, the domain name can provide an idea about the type of organization the creator is associated with, and in many other cases, the country from where the site is originating can be known. As a model, joe@abc.uottawa.ca implies that the individual is likely from the University of Ottawa, which is in Canada. An e-mail address which looks like joe@aol.com or joe@prodigy.com, on the other hand, suggests that the individual is asking people to e-mail him at a private e-mail address.

Another method which helps to find about the creator's background and the file's origin is by looking at the site's URL. Similar to e-mail addresses, the top level domain name in a URL provides information about the creator's organization, as well as the country of origin.

Table 9.1 lists some of the common domain names of the Internet and their meanings.

The URL also provides information about whether the publication is maintained by a department in the organization, or by an individual who

Domain name	Description
.com	for-profit commercial organization
.edu	university or research institution
.gov	government organization
.org	not-for-profit organization
.net	Internet service provider or facility.
.mil	military organization
country codes for countries other than U.S.. such as:	
.ca	Canada
.jp	Japan
.tn	Tunisia

Table 9.1 List of common domain names of the Internet

might have used the organization's system to post his Web page.

Usually, when a URL belongs to an individual, a tilde (~) appears in the site address followed by the creator's name. For example http://www.admin.uottawa.ca/students/~joe, means that web page belongs to a student called Joe from the faculty of administration at the University of Ottawa, which is in Canada. Some URLs however might not be as clear as this URL. By way of illustration, the following address doesn't tell much about the user: http://www.kn.dgbtl/~s664965, nonetheless, it still tells that the page belongs to an individual because of the tilde.

Exceptions to the tilde rule apply when the author is publishing the Web page via a service provider such as the following URL: http:// home.aol.com/joe. This URL indicates that it is an individual's home page because of the service provider's name.

URLs without tildes or service provider name, are most likely published by a branch in the organization, such as http://www.admin.uottawa.ca/mba.htm, which indicates that the site is a top level Web page of the MBA program at the University of Ottawa in Canada.

Even though it is recommended that Internet users, especially students making individual research, stick to sites of well known organizations and entities, such as universities, research institutes like NASA, and information sources like well known newspapers and magazines, many individual publications and Web pages in many instances can also represent invaluable sources of information.

The point is that many Web users are convinced that sites maintained by groups usually mean that information is well maintained and frequently updated. Moreover, having a group of people looking after the site means that more than one individual is interested in the site and that this can imply a longer existence and a higher chance of stability of that Web page than other individual sites.

In order to make their pages more acceptable and attractive, individual page authors should be more concerned about the design and layout of the page. Most importantly, they need to provide users with a certain level of security and assurance that the available information is valid, accurate, and reliable.

Evaluating Credentials

Whether the site is developed by a group of people or an individual, it is important to evaluate the author's credentials and qualifications, in order to warrant the validity and credibility of the received information. The open Internet environment and the low barriers of entry pull in opportunities to those individuals or groups and associations which intend to propagate wrong and/or dubious information, especially those relating to controversial issues.

One method which can assess the accountability and reliability of the material is by looking at the author's job title, history and their educational level. Likewise, verifying if any qualifications (medical, academic, journalistic, etc.) are indicated, lead the reader to expect the author(s) to hold a certain level of responsibility and accountability for the published material.

Many sites provide valuable and valid information, but the lack of qualifications, good design, language skills and information about the author makes the content seem invalid and unreliable. One solution to such cases is to contact the author via e-mail and ask about the sources of the information.

Assessing the Currency and Maintenance of the Information

Knowing how often the information is updated and when it was posted, is an important factor when evaluating Web sites' content. Usually, indications at the end of the file such as "This page is updated every day, week, or month or quarterly etc. " or "This page last updated on..." or "What's new for (month or day)." inform users about the frequency of updates and the recentness of the material. Even in case similar information is not available, most Web browsers have an option such as *Document Info.* in Netscape, which provides information about the file creation and modification dates.

Frequently maintained sites indicate that the Web page is very likely to be stable. It is very common with the Internet that sites come and disappear without notice. For research and educational purposes, it is preferable that users have a certain level of assurance that the site is stable, especially when an instructor is willing to use some bookmarked sites as reference to support the lecture, or when students use them for reference in research papers.

Layout and Design

Well designed and organized sites can significantly help users in assimilating the site's content, and enable them to easily navigate the different links. Design and layout considerations are very important points for a telelearning environment, since Web resources would be a fundamental tool for instructors to support their lectures. The lack of face-to-face contact and real time interaction between instructors and their students requires the use of clearly laid out sites. This would guarantee that the educational message is conveyed, and that users will not lose interest when navigating the site.

The main characteristics of a well designed Web site comprise the following:

- Appropriate use of headings and titles which inform users about the page contents and indicate where they are in the document.
- Fixed navigational elements present in every page of the document to help users return or go to any level of the document at any instant. By way of illustration, including arrow buttons and links to the different sections of the document, including the home site, significantly help to easily navigate the document.
- Ability of understanding the document in text version, without the need of images and graphics. This requirement is of major importance for telelearners with slow Internet connections, who can be frustrated when downloading sites loaded with large graphics, multimedia and photographs.
- Appropriate use of hypertext links. Most importantly, the links must be working and valid.
- Graphics should be informative and not very flashy to a degree which distracts the reader's attention. Graphics should principally aid users in understanding the information or providing options of navigating additional material which could support the information.
- Providing additional links to other relevant information also indicates a well designed site and implies that the site's author(s) wants to help users in assimilating the site's material.

Table 9.2 provides a checklist of elements to be considered when evaluating a web site.

Before proceeding into establishing an Internet based program, a certain number of issues should be taken into consideration by telelearning practitioners, including instructors, administrative staff and students, who should be well prepared to cope with such obstacles.

When it comes to an issue such as security, a virtual institution's strategy should be outlined in such a way that it preserves a degree of privacy and security to the institution's operations, especially for sensitive student related matters such as on-line payments, transcripts and on-line tests and exams.

With regard to policy issues, such as copyright, academic fraud and evaluation of the Web's material, both instructors and students should be

Authenticating the Web site creator(s)
• Is the developer of the site identified?
• Are there any information or links to biographic data about the author(s)?
• If the developer is an organization or association, is there any information about its mission and objectives?
• Is there any contact information?

Evaluating the Web site's content
• Are there any credentials and qualifications?
• How valid and reliable are the credentials?
• How comprehensive is the content?
• Are there any further references and links to additional material and a bibliography which can support readers in understanding the material?
• Is it possible to distinguish between the author's views and facts?

Web site design and layout
• Is the site well laid out and organized?
• Are there any fixed links to help navigating the document?
• Are hypertext links functional?

Table 9.2 Checklist of elements of evaluation of Web material

trained and educated about respecting certain legal and ethical protocols, and to cooperate in creating a competent and reliable telelearning environment. Many other policy issues, however, such as accreditation must be dealt with by the educational institutions themselves.

Bibliography

Books :

- Babbie, Earl. *"Survey Research Methods."* (2nd edition). Belmont: Wadsworth Publishing Company.
- Bates, A.W. *"Technology, Open Learning and Distance Education."* New York : Routledge 1995.
- Information Highway Advisory Council. *"The Challenge of the Information Highway : Final Report of the Information Highway."* Ottawa : Minister of Supply and Services. Canada 1995.
- Kumar, Vinay. *"Mbone : Interactive Multimedia on the Internet."* Indianapolis : New Riders Publishing. 1996.
- Levine Young, Margaret, Levine, John R. *"Internet FAQs™ : Answers to the Most Frequently Asked Questions."* Foster City : IDG Books Worldwide, Inc. 1995.
- Macgreggor, Robert S., Aresi, Alberto, and Siergert, Andreas. How to Build a Secure World Wide Web Connection. *WWW.Security : How to Build a Secure World Wide Web Connection.* Upper Saddle River : Prentice Hall PTR, 1996.
- Robin, Bernard, Keeler, Elissa and Miller, Robert. *"Educator's Guide to the Web."* New York : MIS Press. 1997.
- Sattling, William. *"Mecklermedia's Official Internet World™ Security Handbook."* Foster City : IDG Books Worldwide, Inc., 1995.
- Savetz, Kevin, Randall, Neil and Lepage, Yves. *"MBONE : Multicasting Tomorrow's Internet."* Foster City : IDG Books Worldwide Inc., 1996.
- Serim, Ferdi and Koch, Melissa. *"Netlearning : Why Teachers Use the Internet."* Sebastopol : Songline Studios, Inc., 196.

Periodical articles :

- Bott, Ed. "Online security." *PC/Computing*, September 1996, n9 p344(2).
- Chabrow, Eric R. "Copyright : what's left?." *Information Week*, March 25, 1996, n572, 46-51.
- Giffen, Peter. "The Virtual Classroom." *Sympatico Netlife*, September/October 1996, 15-19.
- "Innovative Teaching Practices." *Accounting Educators : FYI*, May 1996.
- Jafari, Ali. "Video to the desktop and classrooms : The IUPUI IMDS Project. (Indiana

University Purdue University Indianapolis, Interactive Multimedia Distribution System)." *T.H.E. Journal*, February 1996, n7, p77-82.

- Kouki, Rafa, Wright, David. "Internet Distance Education Applications : Classification and Case Examples." *Education at a Distance*. July 1996.

- Kumar, Vinay. "Real-time Multimedia Broadcasts with the Internet Multicast Backbone." *Microsoft Interactive Developer*, February 1997.

- MacIntyre, Blair and Feiner, Steven. "Future Multimedia User Interfaces." *Multimedia Systems*, 1996, n4, p250-268.

- Raynovich, R. Scott. "Tackling Internet Security." *LAN Times*, October 14, 1996, n23, p57-59.

- Schooler, Eve M. "Conferencing and Collaborative Computing." *Multimedia Systems*, 1996, n4, p210-225.

- Schurmann, Gerd. "Multimedia Mail." *Multimedia Systems*, Spring 1996, p281-295.

- Scott, D.F. "The Underground Internet : Through the MBONE, the Internet May Become the World's Largest Broadcast Service." *Computer Shopper*, March 1996, n3, p584-588.

Internet Resources :

- Adobe Systems Inc. "Adobe Acrobat home page."

  [http://www.adobe.com/prodindex/acrobat/main.html]

- Becker, Ralph. "ISDN Tutorial." [http://www.ziplink.net/~ralphb/ISDN/index.html] Last Updated : May 15, 1997.

- Bell Canada. "Bell Z@P ISDN Service.home page"

  [http://www.bell.ca/bell/eng/promo/zap/index.htm] Last updated : April 1997.

- Butler, Brian. "Continuous Education : A Model for WWW Based Education."

  [http://www.umuc.edu/iuc/cmc96/papers/butler-p.html]. April 1997.

- Cable Datacom News. "Cable Modem FAQ." [http://cabledatacomnews.com/cablefaq.html]. Last updated : May 1997.

- Cameron, Donald M., Onyshko, Tom S. and Castell, W. David. "Copyrights, Trademarks and the Internet." [http://www.smithlyons.com/it/cti/index.htm]. November 1996.

- Casner, Steve, Schulzrinne, Henning and Kristol, David M. "The Mbone FAQ." [http://www.mbone.com/mbone/mbone.faq.html] Last updated : April 1997.

- Christopher Newport University. "Christopher Newport University-CNU Online home page." http://cnuonline.cnu.edu/

- Cioffi, John M. "ADSL answers the need for speed." [http://www.internettelephony.com/archive/8.12.96/Features/feature1.html]. Last updated : November 1996.

- College of Engineering, University of Idaho. "Distance Education and the WWW." [http://www.uidaho.edu/evo/dist12.html] Last updated : February 1997.

- CommerceNet. "CommerceNet / Nielsen Internet Demographics Survey." [http://www.commerce.net/work/pilot/nielsen_96/]
- Cornell Research Foundation. "CUSeeMe home page." [http://cu-seeme.cornell.edu]
- Cornell Research Foundation. "Enhanced CU-SeeMe Product Overview." [http://www.cuseeme.com/cu-info.html]. Last updated : May 12, 1997.
- Coyle, Karen. "Copyright in the Digital Age." A talk given at San Francisco Public Library, August 7, 1996. [http://www.nlc-bnc.ca/ifla/documents/infopol/copyright/coyk1.htm]
- Curt. "Curt's High Speed Modem Page." [http://www.teleport.com/~curt/modems.html]
- CyberHigh. "CyberHigh home page." [http://www.cyberhigh.org/]
- DEOS-L mailing List. [http://www.fwl.org/hyper-discussions/deos-fwl]
- Desmond, Michael. "Fast 56K Modems Have Key Drawbacks." PC World Online.[http://www.pcworld.com/hardware/communications/articles/nov96/1411_modem.html]. October 22, 1996.
- Diversity University, Inc. "Diversity University home page." [http://www.du.org/]
- Eckhouse, John. "ISDN-Internet Speed or Digital Nightmare? – The fastest route to the net is also the most frustrating. Here's how to keep from doing a slow burn." HomePC Magazine, September 01, 1996. [http://192.215.107.75/helper/thfeature/featureISDN.html]
- Emerging Technologies Research Group. "Internet timeline : user trends" [http://etrg.findsvp.com/timeline/trends.html]. April 1997.
- Falnagan, William P. "33.6-Kbps Modems : Data in the Fast Lane" PC Magazine Online. [http://www8.zdnet.com/pcmag/features/modems/]. December 1996.
- Fetterman, David M. "Videoconferencing On-line : Enhancing Communication over the Internet." [ftp://gated.cornell.edu/pub/video/html/Fetterman.html]
- Fox, Ken. "MOO-Cows FAQ." [http://www.ccs.neu.edu/home/fox/moo] Last updated, March 20, 1997.
- FOX News Network. "Software Makers Claim Faster Web Browsing." [http://www.foxnews.com/technology/120196/webspeed.sml]. December 1996.
- Gan, Dina. "America's 100 Most Wired Colleges." [http://www3.zdnet.com/yil/content/college/intro.html] May 197.
- Gingold, David. "Cable Modem Resources on the Web." [http://rpcp.mit.edu/~gingold/cable/]. September 1996.
- Graham, Pul. "IRC Related Resources on the Internet. [http://urth.acsu.buffalo.edu/irc/WWW/ircdocs.html]
- Heikkinen, Jyrki. "Secure Electronic Mail." [http://www.tcm.hut.fi/Opinnot/Tik-110.501/1995/secure-email.html] April 1996.
- Huygens, F. "Cryptography and Security Bookmarks." [http://www.ulb.ac.be/di/scsi/book.html] Last updated November 1996.

- Institute for Information Processing and Computer Supported New Media. Graz University of Technology, Austria. "HYPER-G (GENERAL) FAQ COMPLETE." [http://www.iicm.edu/0x811b9908_0x001713cb; internal&sk=599D2238A690]

- Jan C. Hardenbergh, Jan C. "VRML Frequently Asked Questions." [http://vag.vrml.org/VRML_FAQ.html]. Last updated : April 1997.

- JASON Foundation for Education. "The JASON project home page." [http://www.jason.org/]

- Kegel, Dan. "Dan Kegel's ISDN Page" [http://www.alumni.caltech.edu/~dank/isdn/]. Last updated : January 1997.

- Kegel, Dan. "Dan Kegel's ADSL Page" [http://www.alumni.caltech.edu/~dank/isdn/adsl.html]. Last updated : December 1996.

- King, Rachael. "Hurry Up & Wait : ADSL is acing the technology trials. Telcos want to deploy high-speed services ASAP." [http://www.teledotcom.com/1096/features/tdc1096coverstory.html]. November 1996.

- Kumar, Vinay. "The mbone information web" [http://www.mbone.com] Last updated : May 13, 1997.

- Kumar, Vinay. "MBONE Desktop Applications" [http://www.mbone.com/mbone/mc-soft.html] Last updated : April 1997.

- L. Flake, Janice. "The World Wide Web and education." [http://mailer.fsu.edu/~jflake/WWWEd.html]. September 1996.

- Lucent Technologies. "Your Partner for World Class Distance Learning." [http://www.lucent.com/cedl/redblbr2.html] Last updated : March 1997.

- Marcus J. Ranum, Marcus J. and Avolio, Frederick, M. "A Toolkit and Methods for Internet Firewalls" [http://www.tis.com/docs/products/gauntlet/Usenix.html] August 1996.

- Mountz, Mick, Krasnow, Mark, Swistro Chris and Jacobson, Marc. "Cable Modems : Technology, Strategy, and Public policy issues." [http://ksgwww.harvard.edu/~itbspp/proj10/] October 1996.

- Netscape Communications Corporation. "Netscape SECURITY" [http://home.netscape.com/comprod/server_central/config/secure.html]

- NetPhone, Inc. "Netphone home page." [http://www.netphone.com/]

- Page, Melvin E. "Citing Electronic « Materials »... a truly superb guide." [http://www.usc.edu/Library/QF/citing.html]. October 1995.

- Paone, Joe. "Switched Digital : Headed for Decline? : 56Kbps analog modems making managers think twice about ISDN" LANTIMES Online. [http://www.lantimes/96dec/612a035a.html]. December 1996.

- Pollok, Avi. "Canadian Copyright and the Internet." [http://www.ampksoft.ca/compoly.htm].

- Pelczarski, Mark. "Elgin Community College : EDP 205, Visual Programming." [http://courses. Elgin.cc.il.us/vb/]. Last updated : May 6, 1997.

- Pretty Good Privacy Inc. "Pretty Good Privacy home page." [http://www.pgp.com/privacy/privacy.cgi]

- Pretty Good Privacy, Inc. "PGPfone home page." [http://web.mit.edu/network/pgpfone]

- Richardson, Eric. "Site Construction." [http://www.iw.com/1996/04/sitecon.html] Last updated : April 1997.

- Rockwell International. "Rockwell's K56flex Technology Web site." [http://www.nb.rockwell.com/mcd/K56Plus/whybest.html]

- RSA Laboratories, Inc. "RSA Labs : Frequently Asked Questions on Cryptography." [http://www.rsa.com/rsalabs/newfaq/] Last updated May 1997.

- Saltzberg, Steven and Polyson, Susan. "Distributed Learning on the World Wide Web." [http://www.umuc.edu/iuc/cmc96/papers/poly-p.html]. April 1997.

- Savetz, Kevin M. and Sears, Andrew. "FAQ : How can I use the Internet as a telephone?" [http://www.northcoast.com/savetz/voice-faq.html]. February 23, 1996.

- Schneider, Daniel K. "2/3D multi user virtual worlds." [http://tecfa.unige.ch/edu-comp/WWW-VL/eduVR-page.html] Last updated : May 1997.

- Schuler, Cathi. "CeePrompt! Computer Connection : New modems offer easy upgrade" [http://www.ceeprompt.com/articles/102196.html]. October 1996.

- Shin Yamasaki, "Distance education through the Internet." [http://fablink.com/shin/thesis/]. August 23, 1996.

- Scott, Gary. "Distance Learning : All Schools Will Have A Distance Learning Component." [http://www.lucent.com/cedl/dlschols.html]. March 1997.

- SpeedLine Canada, Inc. "SpeedLine Internet Service." [http://www.speedline.ca/Rates.html] October 1996.

- Sympatico ISDN. "Sympatico ISDN : Estimating Costs for ISDN." [http://wwwl.sympatico.ca/ISDN/startup.html]. November 1996.

- Strom, David. "Internet Access : Breaking the Internet Speed Barrier." Windows Sources. June 1996. [http://wwwl.zdnet.com/wsources/content/960617/feature.html]. June 17, 1996.

- Sun Microsystems Inc. "HOTJAVA™ BROWSER 1.0 home page." [http://java.sun.com/products/hotjava/index.html]

- Templeton, Brad. "10 Big Myths about copyright." ClariNet [http://www.clari.net/brad/copymyths.html]. May 1997.

- The Open University. "The Open University home page." [http://www.open.ac.uk/]

- The Globewide Network Academy. "The Globewide Network Academy home page." [http://www.gnacademy.org :8001/uu-gna/index.html]

- Thorne, Steve. "MUDs, MOOs, MUSHs." [http://www.itp.berkeley.edu/~thorne/MOO.html]. Last updated in October 8, 1996.

- Trusted Information Systems, Inc. "Gauntlet Internet Firewall-Frequently Asked Questions" [http://www.tis.com/docs/products/gauntlet/gauntletfaq.html]. Last updated : May 1997.

- Udell, Jon. "Web Conferencing." BYTE, June 1996. [http://www.byte.com/art/9606/sec10/artl.htm]. June 9196.

- UK MICE National Support Centres. "Secure announcements." [http://ugwww.ucs.ed.ac.uk/mice/archive/sdr_docs/node11.html]. June 1996.

- Umass Dartmouth. "CyberEd home pager." [http://www.umassd.edu/cybered/distlearninghome.html]

- Unruh, Bill, "Cryptography." [http://axion.physics.ubc.ca/crypt.html]

- VideoMail Pro home page. [http://www.shout.net/~dtrinka/]

- Virtual Online University, Inc. "Virtual Online University home page." [http://www.athena.edu/]

- Weinschenk, Carl, "The Great Wired Hope." [http://www.teledotcom.com/1296/features/tdc1296modem.html]. December 1996.

- Woolley, David R. "Computer Conferencing on the Web." [http://freenet.msp.mn.us/people/drwool/webconf.html]. May 17, 1997.

- World Transformation. "Cutting Edge Uses of the Web Desktop Videoconferencing." [http://newciv.org/worldtrans/cuttingedge.html]. February 1996.

- Yawer, Nick. "MUDs & Mudding : The complete guide to MUDs and Mudding." [http://www.geocities.com/TimesSquare/6425/]. October 1996.

- Ylönen, Tatu. "Introduction to Cryptography" [http://www.cs.hut.fi/ssh/crypto/intro.html]. Last updated : January 1997.

- Venable, Bryan. "MOO Quick Start" [http://www.missouri.edu/~moo/mooquick.html]. Last updated : May 8, 1997.

- Zappala, Daniel. "ReSerVation Protocol." [http://www.isi.edu/div7/rsvp/rsvp.html]. September 1996.

Index

About the Authors

Rafa Kouki is a Tunisian student presently teaching and pursuing her Ph.D. studies in management at the Faculté de Sciences Economiques et de Gestion de Tunis in Tunisia. She obtained a Master's degree from the University of Ottawa in Canada, where she specialized in Internet-based telelearning and wrote a thesis on that topic. She has worked as a research assistant in The Telelearning Network of Centres of Excellence with funding from Industry Canada. She has an undergraduate major in Management Information Systems and her research interests include innovative computing and telecommunication applications and telelearning.

David Wright is Full Professor at the University of Ottawa, Canada. He has a PhD from Cambridge University, UK and is cited in "Who's Who in the World" and "Who's Who in Science and Engineering". He is a member of The Telelearning Network of Centres of Excellence funded by Industry Canada, in which he focuses on the business benefits of telelearning. He works with private companies and educational institutions to develop business cases for telelearning. He is author of the book "Broadband: Business Services, Technology and Strategic Impact" published by Artech House and has presented papers and chaired sessions at the major IEEE conferences on telecommunications including Globecom, International Conference on Communications and Infocom.